8/10/12

To the lovely
Lesley & Anna.
With love,

xx

AN UNQUIET SPIRIT

AN UNQUIET SPIRIT

The Memoirs and Diaries
of the Artist
Hilary Gialerakis

Edited by Antonia Gialerakis

First published in 2008
Published in 2012 by Quartet Books Limited
A member of the Namara Group
27 Goodge Street, London W1T 2LD
A catalogue record for this book
is available from the British Library
ISBN 978 0 7043 7284 9
Typeset by Josh Bryson
Printed and bound in Great Britain by
T J International Ltd, Padstow, Cornwall

Fiesta, original oil on canvas (mid 70s), is reproduced with permission
as a frontispiece to this edition of *An Unquiet Spirit*

Here in the landscape without horizons
Is the little safety of half-light and possibility –
(The coldness, too, and the fear of half-light and possibility)
Here is perfection, veiled but unassailable

Should I look dispassionately at the careless
foot
So near so delicate a fragment of fulfilment.
Adopt the 20th century malaise of wilful refusal
to care –
Determine to stare vacantly at destruction

Or should I try to preserve my dreams
Simply by turning away.
Preserve the fragment unspoiled; bury illusion
unproved –
Deny life – destroy life out of fear?

Hilary Gialerakis

Foreword
Antonia Gialerakis

My mother, Hilary Gialerakis, born Carter, 1924, lived a colourful, tempestuous life until her death at the age of 79 in 2003.

After a lifetime of illnesses, mystery afflictions and treatment by doctors, psychiatrists and various counsellors from a variety of different disciplines, finally, in the closing chapter of her writings, my mother diagnoses herself as nothing more than an 'unquiet spirit'.

During her many years of pain and very noisy unrest, Hilary was advised to record her story in writing – the lost years, as well as in a diary, covering her immediate experiences. I believe this was done in order to assist doctors and Hilary herself to achieve some kind of clarity and understanding regarding her condition.

In reading this work, we join her on a stormy, but colourful and often very funny journey across the years, from 1924–1973.

Perhaps in writing these memories and the diary, Hilary was seeking to find the answer to her perpetual question: 'What is wrong with me?' – before arriving at this final decision about herself, who she was, and why she was so tormented by illness and pain, imagined or real.

Despite the turbulence of the years, Hilary – who also exhibited under the name of Hilary Lorenzen in South Africa – painted a great many paintings, many of which met with critical acclaim and most of which were sold.

Roger Smith, a family friend who came to live with us for a brief period in 1974 in Umhlanga Rocks, South Africa, wrote to me recently about his memories of Hilary's work as a painter, saying:

'The studio was a delightful space, as I'm sure you remember – the clean, white walls, the tiled floors, the doorway opening out into the bright sunshine, with the bougainvillea cascading down the side. I'm sure it had good light for an artist to work in, whether suffused with reflected daylight or under the electric light when she worked at night, which she was prone to, was she not?

'I fondly remember, at the time when I was staying at Lagoon Drive, how I used to come back from the University (I started my BA degree course that year) and would often go and sit with Hilary in her studio for a while before retiring to my room and my studies.

'I can tell you I much enjoyed these sessions, chatting with Hilary. We would discuss her paintings, and art, and literature. Sometimes she would get me to read to her – mostly poetry (TS Eliot, of course, and others) – but I have a brilliant recollection of being introduced through these readings to Oscar Wilde's children's stories, which sparkle like jewels.

'There's no doubt, looking at the pictures, that they fall into different groups, often with a strong, shared style. The near-realism of paintings like that of The Lotus Eaters; the very geometric, light ones, full of symbolism; the "grey" ones filled with human emotion; the "psychological" ones with stark faces and figures; the geometric, heavier ones, weighed down with pain and suffering; the ones that appear to be simply artist's studies, such as the driftwood and the guitar player.

'Of course there are all sorts of overlaps between these groups, with similar elements and themes cropping up repeatedly. The paintings are also part of an explicit conversation with other artists to whom Hilary was clearly indebted – Picasso, Brancusi, the Cubists, Surrealists and others. But, while we can see the influence of these, I do believe Hilary's work is original and strong enough to stand in its own right.

'Hilary never really discussed these groupings or influences with me, although I did comment to her on some of these aspects and she did not demur. She did sometimes let me in on the thinking behind a picture. I am trying to remember as much of this as I can.

'Some are quite plain – there is nothing subtle about Pain, Gulliver or Sisyphus – but they still have great force. But with others a little background information helped: for example, in the case of the "psychological" painting of the four faces of the individual in a "Johari window": you as you see yourself, as others see you, as you think others see you, and as others think they see you. Hilary took this further, to say there is of course a fifth vantage point, that of the viewer of the painting, who sees it all.

'I have a distinct memory of Fiesta taking shape as she worked on it. She was very professional, you know – quite meticulous in execution, going back time and again to a single element to make careful changes, to get it right. It was certainly like that with this one.

2

'At first glance it strikes one as a distinctly cheerful painting, one of the few in the collection. But is it? There is something a bit manic, frenzied about it, even. That was deliberate, as I recall from a conversation about it with Hilary. The uncontrolled abandonment of the figures to joy is just a little bit scary – and I believe was meant to be.

'In the same style is the painting of the double figure in Night and Day, one rising, the other prone on the floor. The tension between the two is clearly etched. There is a kind of balance between them, but overall the impact is negative.

'The figure on the floor is quite disturbing, particularly in the way the head slides down to the bottom of the picture. It jars, almost as if it is a mistake – but it's quite deliberate, of course.

'Now that I have seen those nightmarish, Dali-esque drawings that you showed me (done by Hilary while undergoing psychiatric treatment), I can't help thinking that it is as if the brains of this figure have been poured out. And yet the picture exhibits a lightness in tone, with the use of white and pale, sandy colours, that it shares with Fiesta.

'Ash Wednesday has to be one of Hilary's finest paintings, because of the precise execution, the strong use of blue, the marvellous tension between the lady and the big cats. It is one of the most memorable. I have a vague feeling that it took some time to take shape and seemed to be in a near-finished condition for a long time before it actually was done. When I first saw it in progress, I could see immediately it was a striking picture.

'But I only understood it when Hilary asked me to read the relevant passages from TS Eliot. There is no doubt they had great significance for her – much greater than I realised at the time.

'I remember how the period of her work mostly at the house in Lagoon Drive [in Umhlanga Rocks] culminated in her comeback exhibition, opened by [the author] Alan Paton. It was a memorable occasion. I remember Paton's speech, how he spoke of the pain in Hilary's paintings and the hope that this had now eased.

'Alas, her paintings did not sell as well as before. Tastes in art in Durban in the 70s were for the likes of Andrew Verster and cool, California-style paintings and not for the work that Hilary had produced, admired though it was.

'I have no authority to speak as an art critic, but I do believe that Hilary's paintings, with their unique style, will find a more receptive audience in London today than they did in Durban back then, especially amid a resurgence of interest in post-war art.'

When my mother posted her writings to me many years before she died, she asked me to read them in the hope that they might bring me to a deeper understanding of her. In many ways they do.

While being both painful and at times shocking for me to read, they are also a lovely reminder of her sense of humour and razor-sharp wit, particularly in her dealings with lovers, family and friends. Through reading this work, the reader does come closer to understanding the 'unquiet spirit' that was Hilary.

When my mother died in 2003, she bequeathed her remaining paintings to me, to ship over to London from South Africa, with a view to exhibiting them in her home country.

Experience of people's reaction to Hilary's art over the years showed me from a very early age that her work instills profound interest and curiosity about the woman who painted these pictures.

Thus in 2008, five years after her death, I was able to put together an exhibition of this work. Alongside the exhibition, I resolved to publish these writings.

Part 1: MEMORIES
Chapter One

2nd April 1924: I am born at Parkstone, Dorset, England (Mama assures me that only heroic willpower saved me from the 1st).

The room is dark, shadowy, without any colour at all. There is a big bed (possibly a four-poster) and a lot of large, dark furniture. In an armchair by the fire is a large shadowy figure (a nurse?) and standing near the door a thin black and white figure. I sense a threat – perhaps from the housemaid who was dismissed for dropping me.

Two years later, I am walking up a path towards the door of a dismal brick house in an endless row of dismal brick houses. Mama's sister, Aunt Doris, is waiting in the doorway. Mama is having a baby, so my sister and I must stay away for a while.

Back home in the nursery, baby Philip stands in his crib with a thermometer in his mouth. I sit on the floor in front of the gas fire and we watch each other. Everything in this room is very clear. All three children live and sleep here.

One day our doctor is sitting on a chair by the window with Philip on his lap. There is something wrong with Philip's neck – it has a big black thing with hairs sticking out of it. Exit Philip – and I learn later that Papa cried and cried and left the house also until he felt better.

Now I am sitting on the floor, playing with bricks. I throw one hard at my sister Felicity's face and she howls. Enter Mama, and my first, unbelievable, smack.

Philip's crib has been replaced by my bed. It is night, but the door is open and the landing light is on. I sit up in bed and vomit a great deal of dark blood. I scream as best I can and Aunt Doris comes in, efficient and reassuring. It seems this always happens when you have your tonsils pulled out.

I am dressed to go out, standing at the top of the stairs. They look very steep and I fall all the way down to the bottom. This is hearsay - I don't remember falling.

Sometimes I walk about the garden and talk to Turner, the chauffeur, and sometimes I watch the children playing in the grounds of the orphanage next door. We visit my mother's family in Tunbridge Wells. A vast ivy-covered mansion, with acres of garden.

I sleep in a large, dark attic, heavily papered with pink and grey roses. There are two pictures I look at from my crib – 'Love locked out' and 'The light of the world'. I see these very clearly still. Grandmother lives downstairs in a wheelchair, where she is to stay for 30 years until her death. She groans and rocks with pain, her hands are all twisted. Visits to her house are always hateful.

Back in the nursery, my sister's bed is under the window. We are supposed to be asleep but the sun is shining and everyone is out. I kneel on my sister's bed, pull back a curtain and watch my parents and Aunt Doris in the road outside. My sister is horrified and tries to pull me away before I am seen. She is a tiresome ass – they will not look up.

They look up and we lie flat in our beds, pretending to be asleep. The door opens and the room is full of large, angry people. My first attempt at deceit has failed, and I am never to so such a thing again.

There is to be a Christmas party for children at Papa's 'works': Poole Pottery, founded by Grandpa and directed by Papa and horrible Uncle Cyril. A fascinating place, with rows of girls painting the pottery that has been designed by lovely, glamorous Aunt Eve, who is later to die of drink.

My sister and I arrive in our new dresses. The room is vast, dusty, with wooden floors, an enormous Christmas tree and countless children standing staring at me. I am violently ill, fall to the floor and am returned in haste and confusion to my nursery.

There is a new doctor now, pleasant and quite unlike the sinister holder of Philip. I am nearly four and I lie in a crib in the garden. I must lie naked in the sun for so long every day depending on what the thermometer says. The garden is nice and I watch the doves and the house.

There is a lot of agitated coming and going. Papa has gone to Switzerland to consult with architects and it seems we are to be going there too. We take the Channel boat and many trains, arriving finally at the Pensione Borgeaud in Chateau d'Oex.

If it is a 'bad' day, I stay in bed. On 'good' days, we visit Mama's friend at the English School and watch our house being built a little further up the mountain. I am taken to the sanatorium quite often. A huge room full of strange things and stuffed animal heads. I lie naked on a cold leather trolley with an even colder X-ray machine pressed against my stomach. It will certainly squash me flat one day.

At last, a Christmas tree is placed on the roof of our house and I am in a new room. I have a little bed beside my parents' very big one, and here I stay. On 'bad' days, I play an endless game with little monkey people made from pipe cleaners by my Aunt Doris. On 'good' days, I am taken upstairs to the schoolroom to be instructed by the governess.

Papa has built such a big house he cannot pay for it, so other sick children are taken in, three or four at a time. The governess and I hate each other on sight. She is disturbing me, and I hear that the children of the Nizam of Hyderabad were good and clever, and the other children here are also good and clever.

I scream all the way to the schoolroom and eventually the governess goes away. A nice, gentle, old lady comes to take her place and I have my lessons alone with her for the next six years. She teaches me many interesting things and I feel that I am reasonably good and clever too.

At bedtime, my father tries to read to me. There is a bad moment coming now when he will get up and wipe his mouth very carefully and kiss me goodnight. I wonder which of us is most embarrassed.

My mother sits on my bed, much too close, and she is crying. I am going to heaven (good - it sounds nice). Or I have been unkind to her again.

I am terrified of the moon, so the curtains must be drawn at night and the door left open. But the curtains are green silk and I can see the moon through them anyway. I dream that there is a luminous green boy under my bed. He lies with his arm right across the gap between my bed and the big one. I can never get out of bed because of him. I see him now, clear as I did then.

The Graf Zeppelin appears soundlessly, filling the sky and the whole valley. I am on the balcony, smothered in rugs, and I cannot move. Will it come back? I shall die of fright.

I lie on the balcony and watch the skaters on the big rink at the foot of our mountain. I am fascinated by little Aly Khan, who is a real

Prince and such a strange and beautiful colour. I watch him through Papa's field glasses and ask my cousin Geoff to take a photo of him for me. I hope for a 'good' day when I may be taken to sit by the rink and see him up close.

Mama thinks I should sleep with the other little girls upstairs in the night nursery, so up I go. Profound dislike is mutual and I hate this room where they keep coming in and out, disturbing me. I hate everything now. I eat boiled fish with horrible black skin that must not be left. I drink horrible camomile tea. My insides have given up the struggle again and Mama advances with the ritual enema. I cry and struggle, but she is large and ruthless and I think she is actually enjoying this. She might at least shut the doors so the other children cannot watch.

Back in my own bed – Mama has given up trying to make me fraternise – and peace is restored. I watch the snow falling outside with delight. I watch the skaters, listen to the music from the rink in winter and the cowbells and the haymakers calling to each other in the summer.

Again Mama thinks I need company, and I am taken to a room at the top of the house and put into bed with Peter, who has recently arrived. Peter is 14 and has terrible asthma. He takes off his pyjama pants and shows me what he has got and what he can do with it. I am astonished and impressed, so Peter says I can do it for him – it should work just as well. It does. I am even more impressed, and for some days we play this game in between Peter's fits.

Now he has a new idea – he will show me what he has seen his Papa and Mama do. It seems they must have enjoyed discomfort and this is not going to work at all. We stand naked and are about to give up when the door opens…

I am returned to my own bed and must never, never do such a thing again. Peter, though still with us, fades, unmissed by me and I return to my own more tranquil games.

Later, Peter's room is occupied by a painter called Francis. He jumps down from one balcony to the next until he lands on mine. He is a splendid young man and I do not mind at all if he sits on my bed.

But, alas, Francis covers the walls with paint and has a tart in the village, so he must go. He jumps once more to present me with his hunting knife, which will be cherished for many years, and he disappears forever. My governess produces a large canvas, paints and brushes, and I paint Eskimos and igloos in the snow. Perhaps I can be a painter too, one day.

I can read for myself now, and do so all the time – my books, Mama's books and some of Papa's books too. My favourite is Sintram and His Companions. I have it still. Sintram is mad, and bad, and very sad. He lives on the mountains of the moon in his castle, and his Companions are Death and The Devil. Eventually he rides the Valley of Death, leaves his Companions there and emerges sane, and good, and happy. My sympathies are entirely with the little boy in the beginning.

I read boys' magazines, play with meccano and wish that I was a boy. One day I am taken to church in the village. There are many children and the Vicar wants us all to sing: 'I am h-a-p-p-y. I know I am. I'm sure I am. I am h-a-p-p-y.' I cannot and I will not sing, now or at any other time in the future. This outing has not done my temperature any good at all and is not, I think, repeated.

I am nine now and the days are mostly 'good'. I walk up the mountain into fields of marigolds and narcissus. I walk down to the village, across the valley, to see at last what is on the other side. There is a wide, wild river, with a suspension bridge. The bridge sways terribly and many of the planks are missing. I must know what is on the other side, so I crawl over, lying flat.

In winter, I can wear a ski suit now, with proper boots, and ride my own luge. Life is very pleasant and full of exciting events. We go for holidays in Italy, to Lake Maggiore, where we drift about in our canopied boat and visit the islands. We sit there drinking chianti and eating cheese (no more boiled fish for me). I wear boy's clothes and I am happy.

We go to Allassio on the Riviera, where my sister and I have a room looking onto a square by the sea. Presently I notice there is a young fisherman down there very often, watching me. He follows us in the streets and lies near to us on the beach. We manage somehow to communicate whenever I can escape alone.

At night, I watch Mama and Papa climbing the steps at the end of the square, heading for the casino. My Romeo emerges from the

9

shadows opposite and stands under my window. His friend is playing a guitar softly and this is all much better than any story I have read. Finally the drainpipe is indicated and he comes. I reach out to help him up – and a bucket of water is poured over us from above, while Mama and Papa are coming down the steps from the casino.

My sister and I lie flat in our beds, pretending to be asleep, but the door opens, and I must never, never, never, never…

As the train pulls out next morning with us on board, my friend runs after it, waving a bunch of tattered flowers. Well, he may be a bad, bad boy, just out of prison, but he certainly has the right sort of ideas for me.

Back home I learn that I must go to school now. VIP doctors in Lausanne have pulled out my appendix, examined me from every angle and declared me fit enough to go. But Switzerland has 'gone off the Gold Standard' once too often for Papa, so we are heading for Portugal, where living is cheap and there is a good English School.

No one, apparently, has noticed that one of my legs has grown longer than the other – walking properly will always be a problem, sports almost impossible and dancing right out of the question. My insides have been damaged beyond repair and there is an S-bend in the middle of my spine: a displaced bone right at the top. I do not know these things myself yet and shall wait for many years to find out why these difficulties are inevitably as they are now.

We take a train to Genoa, a boat to Barcelona (great fun, this) and on to Lisbon. We live in a very small, dark house in a very large quinta, which also has a big house and a farm. It is very hot and dusty: the flowers are brilliant and everything is incredibly dirty, especially Maria the maid. We drink bitter red wine because the water must be boiled or will make us ill. We eat shrimps which dance in the pan as Maria fries them alive. I have a donkey -more or less cleaned up – with a splendid Spanish saddle Papa brings for me. I ride happily about in the quinta, followed by dear Pelitore the ram, who is being fattened up for the farmer's Christmas dinner.

My sister and I go to and from the Good English School in the village taxi. There is a badge on my blazer that says: 'I am. I can. I ought. I will.' Dubious sentiments, these.

I sit in a classroom full of boys and girls. I have not the faintest idea what the teacher is talking about or what to do. Tony, sharing my desk, wets his pants yet again, and we sit staring steadily out of the window, hoping thus to leave this painful scene. My sister, in another room, is happy at last. She has many big, splendid friends, knows what to do and – now she is needed by me – manages to avoid me altogether.

I have cut my finger now and it goes bad. Infection spreads and the nail goes black. I sit in my room with nail scissors, methodically spreading infection to all my other fingers. This is very painful, but most of my hands are bandaged now and I cannot be expected to write.

However, I am still expected to sit in a classroom and listen, so I set to work on my toes. I am taken to hospital in Lisbon, to have the more tenacious nails pulled off with a simple, filthy pair of pliers. I know that I have done this to myself and therefore must not cry. In the next room, Papa is discovered lying flat on the floor in a dead faint, surrounded by astonished nurses. Has the man no sense of occasion? It is I who need consoling for my pain, not he.

However, my feet have been bandaged now, school fades and I lie safely in my bed. Mama, on her way to a party, comes to kiss me goodnight. She has a beautiful dress, smells nice, looks happy. For the first (and last?) time, she is the way a Mama ought to be. I am enchanted and kiss her carefully, but with pleasure.

Papa brings Babette Miranda to the house. Her father is a black man, far away, and her mother is a rough, tough, wild-looking Portuguese. I know that Babette's visits to the house make everyone uncomfortable, but I do not yet know why. My sister knows – she has to walk with Papa every night, being an excuse for him to moon around Babette's house.

We go to Estoril, to the casino. We go to Sintra and walk about in the ancient Moorish palaces. We ride our donkeys in the hills there and admire the peacocks, which are everywhere. This may not be home and it is clearly never going to snow, but it will do well enough.

At night, we clear our beds of fleas with a piece of wet soap, but Mama simply cannot stand them (or Babette?) any longer. Besides which, I am now eleven years' old and really must be sent to school. Papa produces a big blue book describing all the schools in England from which we can choose. We settle for St Christopher's, in Letch-worth Garden City, here described as a 'Progressive, Co-Ed School, where rules are only made by children'. This promises a faint ray of hope somewhere, my parents agree to it and Mama is happy to be going 'home'.

In fact, Papa will settle us and then return to Babette. We take the trains, the Channel boat once more – and Portugal fades out, un-missed by me except for the donkey.

Chapter Two

We now live in a big, ugly house in a wide avenue and I walk along the lanes to the 'progressive' school. The classroom is absolutely full of boys and girls, quite different from any I have seen before. They are not sick or 'foreign' (apart from a few exotic Indian and Nigerian princes), they are genuine 'English'.

I have not even the remotest idea what the teacher is talking about; I can't play netball (though I have to try); I can't make any sense at all of what these children say or do or play. I have long, dark curly hair and during breaks fat, porcine, red-haired Christine swings me round and round by it. She has a piece of wood with nails sticking out of it with which she hammers me while other girls stand round us, cheering Christine on. And so on, and on, and on…

Well, I actually can ride a bicycle and there are many of them in the shed. I take one and ride around the lanes in peace – short-lived because its angry owner lies in wait for my return. I stand up in the middle of the seated class for judgement. 'Why did you do it?' It is impossible to explain this (or anything else much in future, as I shall presently find out). So I stand numb and dumb, looking out of the window. Sam Graves (son of famous Robert) switches off his hearing aid. I switch off everything I have and wait for this to fade.

At home, I have said nothing all this time, but now my sickness and my wounds must be explained. Mama, horrified, speaks to Authority, and now the class is hostile, silent.

I have a brand new, agonising pain and find my pants are suddenly filled with blood. What in heavens name is this? Mama says: 'But I told you long ago. Why don't you take anything in?' 'Will it happen again?' 'Yes, of course, always, all your life.' I am appalled, disgusted, agonised, writhing under the bedclothes. The pain will never go away (and indeed it doesn't, not for a very long time to come).

I have my hair cut very short, acquire a bicycle and spend my evenings in the wood which runs along the back of the houses in this avenue. One evening, Mickey comes into the wood. He is blond and very beautiful and kind and good. He is by far the most popular child in the junior school, has watched it all happening and wants to cheer me up.

We spend our evenings in the wood together now and Mick rides home from school with me each day, carrying my books. Well now, at school, the property of the lovely Mick, I can have any thing or any friend I want. But no, I don't want anything or anyone but Mick. He does my lessons for me and we sit smoking Woodbines, quite contented, in the wood.

We kiss each other softly, playing we are catching toffee-apples, and he teaches me to rollerskate (skates at last, even if they are not proper ones. I can balance much better with them on). This summer holiday we will not part and Mickey rides beside me in the New Forest. We send the groom on ahead and see if we can kiss each other without falling off.

Back home, Mama, in a last (successful) bid to rout Babette, has produced baby Julian. The heat is off. Mick is a darling, and all is well enough. Until… one evening, brother Peter comes into the wood. He is 15 and I know there is something wrong with him, which means he has to sleep with his mother in her bed.

We stare at each other with instant recognition, stare at Mick dismayed, and Peter turns away. I know that he is mad and bad – my heart goes with him, but I see he cannot take his brother's girl. They both fade (for a few years).

I, being 12 now, am walking to senior school. This is really going to be rough. Arriving late, I find the doors all shut and so I open one at random. A group of 19-year-old boys stare at me silently and one, without a word gets up. He opens the window and drops me out into the flowerbed.

I wait for doors to open and am directed to the proper place. I am presented with a stack of papers, which is my work for the month, to be done how and when I like. I am told which classes I really should attend and that I should call teachers by their forenames. This is to show progressive, democratic equality, which becomes more and more plainly ridiculous. I learn to avoid calling the teachers anything at all.

One teacher throws books at us 'beastly little buggers'. Another has got one of the girls pregnant and she is expelled. A big boy hangs himself with a sheet in his hut. A small boy skates into the road and is squashed flat.

In the laboratory, I throw a book at handsome Roger (newly-expelled from un-progressive Harrow and no doubt as confused as I). I am told to stand up for the whole of the double period. Impossible. I shall surely faint. And what price for democracy now?

I should play games – lacrosse now – but, hell, I can't do that to save my life. I take to the woodshed, where ancient, gentle Simon Parker shows me how to make a flute and how to use a lathe. I am content here, making fancy table legs among the quiet boys, who are making a boat. No one will disturb old Simon's reverie, or mine.

In the Paint Room, Francis King pins up my paintings on the wall among 'the best'. But who will do my work now? It seems that cheerful Betty Joseph will, if I will write her essays. When exams come round, I make black marks under my eyes with burnt cork and once in bed send up my temperature by putting the thermometer on my hot water bottle. This trick I learned a long way back and it has never failed me yet.

I do not go to the little wood any more, but to the cinema, two or three times every week, no matter what is showing. Presently a big and really wicked girl turns up, newly-expelled from a convent. She is at once my friend and also has a love in the Post-Matric – a great big, wicked boy, who is always drunk. They ask me to keep watch in the road and disappear together up a muddy little lane. I watch, but when tough Oskar, the Geography teacher, appears, he sees it all at once and goes up the lane…

Another door opens and there is the headmaster, sitting democratically on his desk. A stern and terrifying figure (surely no one calls him Lyn?). Why did I do this? Or that? Or any of the things I have been doing? Impossible to answer or explain, even if I was capable of speech.

At home, I learn that my parents have been asked to take me right away, and so I try – in vain this time – to fade…

Mama needs comfort with her family, so here – in hateful Tunbridge Wells – I stand in front of outraged Aunt Doris. I have caused my mother altogether too much grief – she can't stand anymore and I must go to Boarding School. I picture the night nursery and cry, but she goes on and on…

At home, Papa produces his blue book again and indicates a preference for Dorset. I choose the school that seems as far removed as possible from the last one. It is a small, 'private, Anglo-Catholic Establishment for Young Ladies' in Bournemouth.

Here I find that I must not sit on my bed, walk upstairs in certain shoes, talk in most places, etc, etc. Above all, I must not be found at any time alone or with older girls. I must: play hockey; do endless gym, Greek dancing, Ballroom dancing; run around the golf course directly after breakfast (pain-making bread and jam); dress for dinner (I have no such thing as a dress of this sort); pay attention to lessons; and, above all, pray – twice a day in public and of course most of the time in my thoughts.

My thoughts concentrate entirely on how to evade this whole situation, but the burnt cork routine is ignored here and a 'suitable' girl is detailed to watch me all the time.

I am 13, my hair is short still and I look like a boy dressed up as a girl. I see the Prefects watching me and presently one pulls me into her room and closes the door. It seems she wants to kiss me (Do girls also? Oh yes, indeed they do). She has buck teeth but is a Prefect and so I, astounded, stand quite still.

Presently I find a Prefect I can like – she is by far the kindest and most popular girl in the school and so may save me yet. She does, up to a point, but cannot help with sports, or dancing, or the endless, senseless rules. Our forbidden friendship leads me often to The Study, where I find the sooner I cry, the sooner I shall be released.

I am in trouble now because I will not sing, and stand up in the middle of the seated class… No, I won't sing, or anything else at all that I am supposed to do. My head goes round and round – I fall and do my worst.

I know by now that, although Papa loves big sister best, Mama loves me ferociously, to the exclusion of anyone else at all. I ask to have my weekends at home and Authority (thankfully, no doubt) agrees.

Parents have a temporary house right on the beach, and I – trying to be athletic – jump off the terrace wall onto the hard sand below. My landing knocks the other end of my spine out of joint (for keeps) and I evade school for a little while, until the pain wears off a bit.

But still I jump – this time at night, out of the dormitory window onto the roof, and so down to the ground. I run into the woods to spend a peaceful night alone but have not thought how I can get back again. I can't and so my crime (indisputable at last) is found out. I am to be expelled at once.

At this moment, I am found with whooping-cough and have to be kept after all, up in the sick-room attic. I think this is very funny indeed (they must be mad) and Matron seems remarkably well disposed to me. She even smuggles kind friend Valerie up here to comfort me.

But… Matron is very stout, with a purple face and a grey Eton Crop. She sleeps in the room next door. At night I cough, and cough, and vomit endlessly. Matron appears in incredible yellow silk pyjamas, to sit practically on top of me, holding a basin, stroking my head.

Dear God, I do believe she wants to kiss me too. She does indeed and now I really wish that I was dead. At night, my head under the pillow, I hope that she won't hear me cough, but in she comes…

Mama must get me out of this. Of course, I don't explain, but still she comes and fetches me to cough in peace, alone, at home, and this school – mercifully – fades.

We now have an absolutely enormous, splendid house on the cliffs at Christchurch. There is a big attic with proper, familiar, wooden walls, which is for me.

Parents have acquired a little German-Jewish refugee, Werner, who is to be company for Julian and a good deed for them until his Mama can retrieve him. It seems there is to be a war, but I – not yet 15 – must still be sent to school.

I know there is a big, new, Ordinary High School in the town. Hoping for obscurity, I ask for that, with weekends at home. Papa says: 'Blessed are they who expect nothing, for they will not be disappointed.'

So, with this in mind, I set off for the Ordinary High School. I am directed to a vast, bare dormitory, a new classroom, where to eat. I sit on my bed, pull all its curtains round me and feel absolutely hopeless. This may be Ordinary, but there is a terrible familiarity about it somewhere. More of Papa's words seem very true: 'The more things change, the more they stay put' (he says this in French).

The second night, I feel most a most familiar, agonising pain advancing and I know that this, just now, will be too much. School is too much altogether – it just goes round and round forever.

No one has spoken to me yet, except to teach - my bed is by the door and everyone in here is asleep. I look out into empty miles of corridor, dimly lit with blue lights (black-out now, just in case), roll up my pyjama pants, put on my overcoat and shoes. I know that it is 15 miles to home – I don't wonder what may happen when I get there – I simply have to go. Why? Well, I don't know that – don't even think about it. Do I ever think of consequences? Clearly not.

I reach the empty square – no, not quite empty: there is a policeman there. He wants to know where I am going. 'Home, sir, just up there.' Conviction wins (this was more or less the truth) and he lets me go on.

It is getting light now and my feet are bleeding, blistered rags. But I am not far from home and crawl through a garden, through a river, down onto the beach, where my feet will not be noticed. Presently I walk right into the sea (why?). I see a familiar bit of cliff, a familiar postman riding along the top on his motorbike, I fall flat in the sand once more and pass out altogether.

I don't remember Postman carrying me home in his sidecar, but he does, and presently I wake up in Mama's bed. My feet are boiling, bandaged lumps – my body aches and my head is falling off – but still, I made it and these pains will pass. But someone is sitting on a chair beside my head.

I take a cautious look – well, now I'm truly lost. I can't believe it, but it is most certainly the Head. I close my eyes,pretending to sleep – I try to fade – but no, my tears are giving me away. 'Why? How? Why?' again. No one, in all her years at school has ever done such a wicked thing before. 'Why? How?' Well, I lie there, dumb and sobbing, until at last, outraged, exasperated, she goes away.

Next day I learn that I am going to be taken to a psychiatrist. What is that, then? Well, you'll see. A sort of doctor, who will fix you up.

Dr Odlum is very, very stout, has a purple face, a grey Eton Crop. I am at once a sopping, sobbing, mess. The questions go on and on and on, and she winds up by stating, very firmly, that a good Game of Hockey is all I need and that will fix me up.

At home, I agree I will go back to school, but only daily, on the bus. In this way I can hope to avoid Dr Odlum, and Hockey, and the dormitory – it should do well enough. Back in the classroom everyone stares and I stare out of the window, looking forward to the bus. I avoid Scripture with the Head (she's had another go at me meanwhile). I avoid practically everything, in fact, and so am ignored totally.

At home, my parents sit listening to the news most of the time. There really is going to be a war, they think.

But first we go for holidays to Letchworth: Mick and Peter - good! This is great fun. Mick is big and handsome now, but I lie in a cornfield watching Peter at his easel, painting, as often as I can. Mick comes home with us, but soon there really is a war, announced and definite, so he goes home, taking my accordian for a last, sad, regretful souvenir.

Well, I really can't go to school now (the bus might me bombed). I am 15, not quite illiterate, and school, for me, is over.

Chapter Three

For the next few months, everyone is very excited, wondering what this war is going to be like. They listen to the news, and Johnny crosses the road to ask if he may play tennis with me, on our court. Desperation taught me, at The Establishment, to make an absolutely unreturnable service, which meant I could win every other game outright, standing still.

Johnny is about 18, very dark, very elegant in his velvet jacket, quiet, very gentle… Good: I am pleased to see him. We do not play tennis - we sit up in a tree, out of sight, and talk. He is making harpsichords and in the evenings he visits me, bringing a red rose from his garden.

If it rains, he plays the piano and we are always left alone together since he is clearly a very 'desirable' young man and is keeping me out of mischief. We have a lot to talk about (Johnny has the most awful troubles too) and are reasonably convinced that we shall love each other for ever and ever…

Papa is mostly in London, looking after Austrian refugees, and one day he brings one home for a visit. Litzi is about 18, very plain (Babette at least was beautiful) and very worthy. Papa and Litzi sit under the oak tree in the middle of the lawn, holding hands and looking altogether ridiculous. They call each other David and Debora (who were they? I still don't care to know).

Mama and I watch them from the window in disgust – she says he is a silly old fool and always was. When she married him, he thought babies would come out of her navel! She had to send him to a doctor to be told what to do. He is absolutely hopeless still and should have been a monk.

I picture Papa as a monk and see that in fact a monk is the only thing he happily could have been. However, Mama is going to retaliate with Pauline, a ghostly, drooping figure, who broods over the piano when she is not shut up in the bedroom with Mama.

I see dimly that there is 'something wrong' about Pauline, but she plays most splendidly all the current hits from Radio Luxembourg for me, and the Moonlight Sonata, endlessly, for Mama, taking Mama's attention away from me.

One evening Pauline sends an SOS. Her brother, a Vicar, has locked her up in the vicarage so that she cannot visit Mama any more. Mama is in a terrible state – Pauline must be rescued at once, immediately.

Parents and I pile into our enormous Sunbeam and plunge out into the night, heading for Wells. The night is packed with drama, but the vicar wins the round and we return alone. Pauline appears again later, dressed as an ATS officer – the call-up saved her and she clearly was not as wet as I had thought.

There is a lot of trouble now with little Werner. He calls constantly for his Mutti, cries a lot, cannot speak or understand any English, and finally bites Julian as hard as he can. Papa picks him up very roughly and locks him, sobbing bitterly, in his room.

I – having always thought Papa a kind though foolish man – am absolutely shattered. This is the most unfair thing I have known to happen yet and it is to have considerable consequences.

I notice now when Mama points out to visitors her little 'Jewish refugee'. I notice that he only has what Julian doesn't want, does only what Julian wants to do and is treated really quite atrociously. I hate both parents now most bitterly: I am ashamed of them, dislike Julian and devote myself a lot to Werner, who is in fact a very gentle, clever, pretty little boy.

Now our cliffs are mined, the beach is covered with concrete tank-traps, there is a mysterious 'death ray' machine (radar!) hidden in the trees nearby and an aerodrome right behind our house. Cook says Hitler is 'consecrating' his troops on the frontier. Johnny has gone off to be a pilot in the Fleet Air Arm. Even Alvar Liddell, reading the news on the BBC, sounds just a little ruffled.

Standing in the garden, I look up to see an enormous aeroplane apparently about to cut off the top of our oak tree. I see black crosses on its wings instead of the now familiar rondels and am considerably ruffled myself.

Parents - horrified - say 'they' are after the aerodrome and we shall go up with it. We are in the worst, most dangerous place that we could be. Cook, alarmed at last, takes off with her fireman. Nanny takes off with her milkman. Parents, little boys and I pile into the Sunbeam and head off for Wales, where we shall be safe, they think. I am very sad indeed. I thought this was home.

Wales has black, gloomy mountains and a narrow, wild river that runs right through the middle of some village with a totally unpronounceable name. The natives are dark, gloomy, hostile... Wales will not do at all.

We re-cross the border and come to a remote, stark, absolutely hideous farmhouse. I have to sleep in a vast, awful feather bed with Mama. The farm, the farmer (there was 'something wrong' about him but I don't remember what) are even worse than Wales.

Papa has lost sight of his money again (it is 'all tied up') so we go south, to Kidderminster, to a very small private school where Mama is to do housework for our keep and the little boys are to be educated.

Kidderminster, the school, and the Head, are all grey, wet, unbelievable, unrelieved misery. All four of us sleep in one big, bare, dirty room and Mama is promptly ill and takes to her bed. I am really sorry for Mama at this point.

Well, someone has to do the housework, so I will see what I can do. I learn to lay the fires, sweep the rooms, dispose of revolting balls of greasy, grey hair (from the Head) and whatever is to be found, in pots, under all the beds. I also have to 'answer the door', which is worst of all since I am painfully aware that, in filthy pants and jersey, I do not look like the housemaid I am supposed to be. People will stare, I think – and so indeed they do.

Eventually I am even sicker than Mama, so she gets up and has a shot at it. But now Papa, more or less solvent again, comes to the rescue: he has got a small 'pre-fab' house near Evesham for us.

But at some stage about this time we were also at Broadway in the Cotswolds. I remember a beautiful house, young Olivier painting in the garden in a topless hat, and a lot of bombs falling nearby one night.

Well now, in our clearly temporary pre-fab, we must do something about the war. There is a large WVS van, and Mrs Whitford, in uniform, drives this with Mama beside her and me in the back with urns of tea, cakes and cigarettes. We visit the searchlight stations, gun-sites and aerodromes, providing comfort for the troops. The soldiers and the airmen are always very pleased to see us, and I can (and always shall) get along very well with them.

Mama now has a Warrant Officer from the nearest aerodrome and I don't like this at all. He is uncouth and has no business to be sitting on the sofa with his arm around Mama. How can she? I wonder dimly where they propose to spend the nights and hastily remove my belongings from Mama's bedroom to the little hut in the garden.

I have an absolutely gigantic soldier with a very round pink face, who would not dream of even holding my hand. He just wants a place to go when he is off duty and someone to talk to about his young lady in Newcastle. Johnny turns up on leave, dressed up as an Able Seaman with a beard. He is doing it the hard way, like his father the Commander did.

Thus disguised, he might as well have come from Mars and we have nothing to say to each other at all. He can't tell me what he is doing, or even where, and my mind is more or less a blank. Papa appears again, with news of a proper house for us in another village, also near Evesham, and once again…

A really beautiful house now, hundreds of years old, with a thatched roof, beams and all. It is a bit spoiled by having a newer bit stuck on to it, but this is to be occupied by our 'billetees'.

They are a family from Hong Kong. The husband is very tall, dark and handsome. Very smooth. He is a radio announcer and is having an affair with one of his female colleagues. His wife is a haggard, red-haired beauty, 20 years older than him, who plays the piano a lot, smokes endless cigarettes in an endless holder, is never seen without her sable coat, and is perfectly charming to the female colleague. I admire everything about her very much.

They have a little girl and a Chinese Ahma, who is having a hard time so far from home. Poor Ah Fung, in white jacket and black bell-bottoms, is stared at if she goes out at all. She is saving up to buy a baby when she goes home and keeps all her money in a sort of bandage tied round her middle, which makes her look stranger still.

She looks after the little girl and dutifully laughs away whenever Master bangs his head on the low doorways! He swears terribly at her then, but she laughs on and I want to know why. A Chinese custom, he says – it is done to cheer you up whenever you hurt yourself.

All this is pleasant enough, but… I have learned to skin rabbits now and cut them up just right for cook. I find, with somewhat horrified surprise, that I enjoy doing this very much. We eat rabbits all the time now, and drink the cider they make in the village.

Poor Werner, now about four, is having a worse time than ever. He does not want to eat now, and mealtimes, when he is forced to do so, are a torture to us both. The governess is clearly on Werner's side but of course cannot oppose Mama.

Werner cries more and more, while I protest more and more violently. One night, I fetch my big, sharp, rabbit-cutting knife and stand with it looking at Mama, sleeping in her four-poster. I think she is not fit to live and, if I can cut up rabbits, why not her? I stand there a long time, looking, but I just can't do it after all.

However, I take Werner's bed into my room now and him into my bed with me. I protest about absolutely everything now and say Werner must go back at once to Mutti. So he does, a few weeks later. I must have made a lot of fuss about this.

I think now how I can get out of here as soon as possible. Everyone, I know, wants shorthand typists, which should do until my call-up. So I buy a book about how to do shorthand and settle down with this in the kitchen, until I can more or less keep up with whoever is reading the news.

I also go to Evesham to learn typing and to be sure my shorthand is going to be fast enough. The instructor at this office wants me to stay and teach others, but I want to go as far away as possible. Of course, I have no money of my own until I earn some, so I must still depend on Parents' wishes to some extent. We compromise, finally, with the proposition that I shall go to Papa's cousin Herbert, who is usually Lord Mayor of Poole, always a JP, and can be relied upon to keep an eye on me (I know him and I know he won't).

And so, nearly 16, and in some ways not quite uneducated, I return to Parkstone, Dorset, hopefully intending to Live My Own Life.

Cousin Herbert's house – well named The Hermitage – is on a hill overlooking Poole Harbour. I ask for a room at the top of the tower and from here I watch Johnny going round in his Walrus seaplane being shown how to fly. I watch a train down there being machine-gunned one night and 'them' trying to blow up the gasworks (I know it is a dummy – the real one is somewhere else altogether).

Downstairs Herbert, his wife (my father's sister, Maude) and I sit at one end of half a mile of table for meals. This is about the only time I ever see them. I watch for Herbert turning off his hearing aid, as Maude talks on and on. He then disappears into his study, followed by his goat, Nellie. Maude, bereft of servants, has so much to do that I am left alone to think, up in the tower.

But I am soon bored in this uneventful house. Herbert will not take me out in his enormous yacht, and this is not what I had in mind at all. Presently Maude says there is a 'suitable' job for me not too far away down the hill. It seems that Hazel Buckland, a Psychiatric Social Worker, known to Maude, is in need of a secretary and that is what I am to be.

I find a pretty little cottage, open the door, and see Hazel coming downstairs in a rush, on her way out. Am I the new secretary? Well then, here is the appointment book, there is the telephone, and will I please make appointments for…

At this time I have never used a telephone in my life, have never seen or heard of an appointment book – have absolutely no idea whatsoever what it is or what to do. I want to turn around and run, but stand there shaking, waiting to be dismissed. Hazel stares at me – incredulous, exasperated – and finally takes me upstairs to her room.

This room is absolutely full up with Hazel's bed, everything she possesses and everything connected with her work. She clears a bit of windowseat for me, points out a typewriter and a stack of papers I can copy out, and says she will be back later.

I find that the typewriter is American, with all the letters in the wrong place, and that the papers I am to copy are case histories. I start to type them out, with one finger and growing interest.

Hazel comes back much later and finds out that I actually can type, do shorthand, but am quite petrified of the disembodied voice which comes out of the telephone, which she is now patiently trying to show me how to use. She gives this up and sits on her bed asking me questions softly, kindly, so that presently I look up and see her.

I see that she is not much bigger than me, has very black, short hair, very wise, brown eyes, a rather yellow face with a lot of lines, and definitely 'odd' clothes. I also see that she is by far the most satisfactory person I have met in my life and that she is not going to kick me out after all.

The next day we drive off together to the Hospital where she works for two psychiatrists. Their names are Dr Statham – and Dr Odlum. Oh dear, I think. Well, perhaps she won't see me. Dr Odlum and I are confronted by each other in the outpatients' hall and refuse to recognise each other at all.

But Hazel sees something the matter, so I tell her and am left in future in the car outside to type case histories on my lap. I talk to Hazel a lot, mostly in the car, and presently she says I should talk to Dr Statham. Years ago he fixed her up and she thinks he is very nice and very clever.

To please Hazel, I go twice a week to Dr Statham's house for the next year. His house is very large and grey. He is very small and grey (a little grey sheep, with glasses). I lie on his divan and invent answers to most of his questions, until, determined to get at the truth, he decides to hypnotise me. He sits behind my head now – thus obliterating himself altogether – and I hold a little stick with a ball hanging from it on a piece of string. I am to notice that it will go round and round whichever way I will it to, while he talks on and on. I see with some alarm that it actually does and that in fact I may go helplessly to sleep.

At home, locked in my room, I make something similar and find out how this really works. Then, back in his dim room, I swing it round, invent more answers and stare out of the windows. Who, after all, would want to talk to such a disembodied, chilly, little ghost? I am, here, a case history. He is simply not there at all. But still I go, to please Hazel.

Meanwhile, Mama has come back, with Julian, to live in the top half of a house nearby, exactly opposite the house I lived in as an infant and where Philip died. This could not be more dismal than the Hermitage and so I join them there, while spending as much time as I can with Hazel.

In a small, bare, room next to Hazel's room lives Dr Kitty Andrews. She is tall and gaunt, has short grey hair, looks very stern and often puts her head around the door when Hazel is out, to see if I am all right. Hazel says she writes poetry, besides being a doctor, but I simply don't believe this until one day Hazel, smiling faintly, gives me a page from Argosy magazine that has a poem, written by Dr Andrews, about me. Their actual relationship – now perfectly obvious – never crossed my mind at all, in spite of my experiences at The Establishment.

One day, Hazel says I must be a witness at court against a female case history who has stolen (once too often) something from her car. I don't want to do this at all, for many reasons, but since I did watch this happen (saying and doing nothing) and Hazel says it will be the best thing to do, I face the court and stutter, more or less, what I have seen.

The next time I am outside the hospital I get out of the car and go into an arcade nearby. There is a bookshop here with some books outside. I take one of these, at random, and go back with it, undiscovered, to the car.

Hazel has a cash box in her room, and now I take money from that, most days, knowing she is bound to know and wondering what she will say. Presently she says that the delinquent girl who does the housework here has once stolen her gold watch, and that she – finding it in the kitchen – gave it to this girl to keep for herself. I see what she is getting at, but continue to steal from the cash box all the same.

Besides the girl in the kitchen, there is often another girl in the house. She is a female case history, who now comes into the room where I sit on the windowseat writing (only letters now) for Hazel. This gaunt and filthy hag has cut off both her breasts and says she has got shrapnel in her (toothless) gums. She shows me all her awful wounds, day after day, babbling with delight, until Hazel – very angry – chases her away. I find she is a 'paranoic' and hope that this, for me, will be 'the one that got away'.

In the evenings, after dinner, I go out into the park to find the soldiers, sailors and airmen who are always there. I walk about with one of them (never the same one twice) every evening and listen to them talking about their real lives at home. My real life is clearly impossible, so I invent various more suitable lives for me and talk about them.

Mama is now distraught, convinced I am 'going on the streets'. Well, if she wants to think the worst I shall not even try to explain that my companions only walk and talk with me, holding my hand usually, and sometimes leaving me at the gate with an entirely brotherly goodnight kiss. Mama goes for help to Hazel, and either Hazel or Dr Statham tells her to leave me alone over this.

Now Johnny comes on leave again, looking much more like himself in a very smart uniform with lots of gold braid. Mama leaves this 'suitable' young man alone with me, and presently he pulls me hard up against him and, well, what is he doing? Finally he goes into some sort of fit, stops dead, looks very cross indeed and disappears into the bathroom. I see, very dimly, remembering Peter and his fits, no doubt, what this may all be about. But I cannot imagine why he always ends up so bad tempered, so unlike his distantly-remembered self.

Returning to the park, I find Canadians now, who are pleased to talk French with me but are otherwise exactly like all the others here. One evening a civilian meets me in the park, lies me down in the reeds beside the lake, and becomes very un-brotherly indeed. I now find out exactly what Johnny was up to and a good deal more besides. Still remembering young Peter's games, I know what he wants – all he can get, anyway, since there are always many people around the lake.

At this point Mama takes Julian and I away for a holiday to some village, on a cliff. I see a narrow ledge down the face of the cliff and consider that, if I climb down there and wait until it is dark, I inevitably shall fall off and so end the hopeless confusion of my life at last. The cliff is very steep, the night very dark indeed, and my ledge narrower even than I thought. I wait there for hours and hours, listening to Mama calling, calling... Finally – I don't know how – I climb back up the cliff to lie sobbing, defeated, on the grass at the top.

Back in Parkstone, now nearly 17, I decide not to wait for the call-up. I can volunteer and be trained for something until I am 17. I want the Navy, but have no matric (not even School Certificate, in fact) so I will try for the RAF.

I take a bus to the right place and find an enormous tent in which I see many doctors, answer many questions and have various tests. The last doctor, who will decide my fate, looks through these results, looks at me and says if he was my father he would keep me right out of the war altogether. He writes out a document which says I am C3 – totally unfit.

Now at home or with Hazel, I find that I can't go out much anymore at all (everyone is staring, staring). I lie in bed a good deal, with an awful pain, stop even pretending to work and refuse to talk to anyone (Dr Statham has given up by now). I fall about and break one of my toes, which still hangs loose today and will cause more pain and trouble walking all my life. It does, too. Right now.

One day, I find Hazel sitting somewhere near me and I hear her saying that she wants me to come with her to London, where there is a very special doctor who will help me. I surely feel there is not much for me to lose and so I go with Hazel in a train to London to see Dr Lambert.

Dr Lambert's waiting room at his surgery appears to be made entirely of silk and Chinese pictures. Warm, comfortable and softly lit. I open one eye to look at this, but all the same expect the worst.

Presently someone takes me to the room next door – a very comfortable study this, all lined with books. The curtains are always drawn, so you can't look out of the window. Dr Lambert sits with one foot on his desk, one hand supporting his colossal head, in a huge, carved chair. He really is a very big man indeed, very dark – an exaggerated Orson Wells, in fact. Not a little grey man, but definitely someone very real.

No use to fabricate then, when the questions start. I hear a deep, soft, Austrian rumble and answer on and on – the truth now, as far as I know it at that time. But the truth is very painful and of course I end up in tears. Will I ever stop?

I hear Dr Lambert sigh and see him sitting on the desk now, pulling me out of my chair. 'A difficult life. Go ahead and cry, kid, but please notice that this is a very expensive suit.'

My head, now resting on a solid, beautifully perfumed, rock, will soon begin to stop revolving. The rest of me, held firmly up against more solid rock, will soon stop shaking. I cry some more (regardless of the suit), but only with relief now, and very soon there is nothing left to cry about. Dr Lambert starts telling stories about old Vienna.

Well, now I know that someone knows exactly what it is I really wanted all along – and ever really shall want. Dr Lambert sits there, brooding, smoking, for a while – then cleans me up a bit and returns me to my chair.

He has made up his mind. I must go home now, collect what I want and come straight back with Hazel, to the mental hospital at Mill Hill, where he will come to see me. He talks to Hazel while I wait, fast asleep on the sofa, next door. At 'home', I find that there is nothing much I want at all. I leave again (this time in a sense forever) with Hazel, for Mill Hill.

This was a public school for boys but is filled now with soldiers dressed in blue. We go down the hill a little way to a big old house where civilian women are kept. It looks quite ordinary on the outside. In the hall now, I see Hazel standing in the doorway looking back at me over her shoulder. She is looking very upset indeed, says nothing at all, shuts the door and disappears.

The hall is vast, quite bare and very, very dirty. There is a lot of noise – people screaming, crying, shouting. I had expected case histories but nothing like what I see and hear around me now. I try to picture Dr Lambert in these surroundings, fail completely and give up altogether.

Presently I come to – briefly – to find myself in a bed in a big, bare, dirty room with other people, also in bed. Someone gives me two very small kittens and tells me for God's sake to shut up. The kittens go into the bed and my head goes under the pillow. It is night now, but the light is on and I see a girl, even younger than myself, fighting furiously in the middle of the room with three men in white uniforms. Two are trying to hold the girl while the third tries to give her an injection. She is making a very great deal of noise indeed – appears to have fantastic strength – but ends up senseless on the floor.

Hereafter, my first concern must be to make myself as inconspicuous as possible. The next morning, I am dressed, moved to another room upstairs and taken somewhere else to do an IQ test. I know what this is, more or less, but am surprised to find mostly just a lot of patterns, with perfectly obvious faults, which I can rearrange in relative peace and with some interest.

We eat in the cellars – more noise again, and someone falls down hard, foaming at the mouth. Another patient rolls her over, with a spoon between her teeth and sits on her until she is still. The nurses ignore this sort of thing altogether and never speak to me except to give directions.

That night, in a long, bare, filthy room with about 20 other people, I lie in bed smoking (about 75 a day here, since sleep is brief and there is nothing else to do) and wait for the air-raid sirens to start up. In the next bed, a greasy skeleton drinks from the bottle she keeps under her pillow and presently she starts up, laughing, babbling nonsense.

When the bombers start coming over, the noise is really indescribable. People dive under their beds and lie there, screaming, while the bombs crash on and on. The bombers roar overhead, our dim lights flicker, I am very cold indeed, so under the bed will be worse than in it. 'They' can drop whatever they like on this place, the sooner the better.

My bed is by the open door and presently I see a nurse there, shouting at me over the din to come out and hurry. She pushes me into a little room, right next door. There, incredibly, is Dr Lambert, quite unruffled, even smiling a bit. Presently I look at one raised, enquiring eyebrow: 'So? Well, come here, kid. No need to stand there catching a cold, looking for trouble…' So now I can believe anything and shall not cry much anymore, or fall to pieces, for the next six years at least.

The noises fade away and I answer questions, on and on, in comfort. Presently I ask one myself: was my IQ any good? 'Yes. Far too good for comfort.' Hazel tells me later it was 175, but I don't make any sense of this – either then or now. I continue answering questions until the All Clear sounds and I go back to bed.

During my stay at Mill Hill, Dr Lambert wanted to operate on my head, but my father refused permission for this. Electric shocks were then suggested but also refused by my father. Mill Hill was an 'experimental' hospital. I do not remember who told me these things, or when, but think it was either my mother or Hazel, a long time later.

Life at Mill Hill has some unpleasant surprises for me too. I see dead people being taken away at night. People being forced to walk when they can't do it. An apparent corpse lying in a dark room, being fed fantastic stacks of potatoes. People with their arms and legs broken from their 'shock treatment'. People having endless fits. The nurses' total disregard for all these things.

Dr Lambert does not come here very often. He says far too many people are making far too much fuss about this war. His 'Park Lane Poodles' are constantly in hysterics and he is obliged to rush about all over the place. The bombers come round us, so everyone expects to burn to death, which will be worse than simply being blown up. The noise gets worse and worse, and there is simply nowhere one can be alone here.

After two or three months of this, it seems to me I have to go. Where? I have no idea, and only think of how to do it. I have a friend of sorts here, Stella. She is about my own age, long red hair, dead white, dead set face and a peculiar, jerky way of moving. She hardly ever speaks, but we spend some time together, smoking, staring, doing nothing. She looks about the way I feel and presently we decide to bolt together.

I have noticed how a girl in my room manages to escape most nights to visit the soldiers at the big hospital. Stella knows how to get right into London, has someone she thinks she can go to there, and is willing to try.

So, one night, we go off together while the nurses are safely eating in the cellar. We spend this night in the deserted stables of the big hospital, buried in the hay, and in the morning we set off for London, hoping to get right away from Mill Hill Mental Hospital forever.

Chapter Four

Stella and I take the Underground to Hampstead, to Dr Winnicott in Pilgrims Lane.

Dr Winnicott is a psychiatrist for children, clearly very well known to Stella, and he greets us very kindly indeed. Stella disappears with him while I sit by the fire admiring a perfectly beautiful panel on the wall.

Presently he comes back to sit and talk with me. What was I doing in Mill Hill? Thinking hard, I can't really imagine, but say at last that 'I just mistook my direction'. He says this is a very good answer, asks a bit more and then goes off to telephone (presumably to pacify anyone at Mill Hill who may have noticed our absence).

Stella comes back with the Hampstead newspaper and shows me where to look for a room. She stays with Dr Winnicott. Kingswell House looks promising, so I set off down Primrose Hill to look for it, with the few possessions I have.

I find two big houses stuck together in a very pleasant street, Pond Street, near the heath. The Roebuck Inn is on one side and Julian Huxley is on the other (I one day see him leaning out of his window, throwing a pair of socks down at his wife in the street).

The front door is hurled open and there I see Miss Beatty - very large, draped in a kaftan. She has short, grey hair, a purple face (never mind - her lady friend looks after the annex). She looks formidable, but I say what I have to say – that I have hardly any money at all but I will pay her when I can if she has, please, got a room, any sort of room? She stands there glaring and presently bellows, 'Come on then!', and plods off up the stairs until we come to the very top. She flings open a door and there is absolutely the most perfect room I could possibly imagine.

It is a little attic, with a very steep roof, bed, table, chair, cupboard, gas fire and a mat. Miss Beatty says it is 37 shillings and sixpence a week, including breakfast, supper and laundry. Mr Parkes next door will show me how to work the hot-water geyser and tell me when and where to eat.

Do I have a parent? I recall that Papa also lives in London, mostly, and produce a letter to prove it. Miss Beatty, satisfied, goes off to leave me to admire my room in total, unqualified, bliss. Writing this now, I see that Miss Beatty must have kept a number of the people I find here for nothing at all. I wonder if Dr Winnicott played some part in my apparently miraculous good fortune here.

Presently I find Mr Parkes, a cheerful young man who is going off to be a Padre in the RAF (to be shot dead in his first week there), who gives me his socks to mend while he tells me what to do. He shows me how to deal with a London geyser with the best chance of it not blowing up while you are actually in the bath (they always do, no matter what).

After supper, he leads me to the cellar as the sirens start up nearby. This cellar is big and bright and full of people, laughing, talking, playing games. A Polish boy sits there playing the piano and Miss Beatty stands in her kaftan delivering a most passionate oration about Albert Schweitzer, whose portrait hangs here on the wall. Thus, fully occupied between Warsaw and Darkest Africa, the noise outside goes unnoticed until the All Clear, when Miss Beatty leads us back upstairs to kick incendiaries away from the house.

They roll away down the hill onto the heath. So who said these things would burn you to death? 'They' can do what they like – have no chance at all against Miss Beatty – and in future will be ignored by me altogether. Most people here sleep on the floor in the cellar, but I – recently put off even the nicest cellar – never go into one again, and spend the rest of the war in various attics.

In the morning after my first day, I ask for directions to Mayfair and – after some difficulties with the Underground – find the right door to Dr Lambert's rooms. He is coming downstairs in a rush, in a black coat and homburg, on his way out. 'So there you are. Better come with me.' We fall into the waiting taxi and take off at great speed. He is not annoyed by my abrupt departure from Mill Hill but wants to know how on earth…? This simple matter explained, he is ready to listen to my latest achievements and to agree that these are satisfactory.

Back in his room, he gives me a very long talk (which I don't remember clearly), some pills to take at night (Seconal), some pills to take during the day (Benzedrine), and tells me he is going to speak to Papa. He also says that in future I must turn up between 6 and 10, when he sees people ('artists and such') for nothing.

I shall find usually congenial company in the waiting room at that time. I am please to stay put in Kingswell House, of which he knows, and learn to use the telephone.

Back in my room, I see Papa talking to Miss Beatty. I do not remember much of what we say to each other, but it is agreed he will give me money until I can find work. I do not like this much.

Stella turns up and takes me into the pub next door, where there is a splendid fire and many cheerful people. We sit by the fire, drinking dark brown ale and looking in the newspaper for something I can do. I know quite well that I am 'mental' and therefore should not try to use my head.

For this reason, I take a job at the Medical Research Institute at the top of Primrose Hill, where I am to clean the cages of the rats and mice kept there for experimentation. This job is not hard to get and I am shown how to pick up the rats by their tails so that they cannot bite me (they do anyway). If you do not hold their tails very hard, the rats will shed them on the outside and fall to the ground with bleeding, raw remains.

There are thousands of rats and mice to clean out every day, and the dogs and monkeys in other rooms scream and howl with pain every day, all day. It is a very terrible place, and presently I start to choke the mice to death – more and more every day. Why? I don't know why, but only that I have to do it, and the world is getting dark again.

While this is going on, one day while I am waiting in the hall for supper, I notice everyone around is talking about a man who comes in most evenings, from the annex, to use the telephone. Miss Beatty is very polite to him, calls him 'Mr Frees' and is positively deferential. He always wears a long black coat and a black hat – and never speaks to anyone except Miss Beatty. Everyone speculates about this entirely fascinating stranger.

One night, overcome by hunger, I go down into the hall to see if I can steal a piece of bread. Miss Beatty has 'views' about food, which means it is mostly raw vegetables, which I cannot eat, however hungry. I think that everyone must be asleep, but – as I am eating the bread – the front door opens and there is the mysterious, really terrifying Mr Frees.

I stand there quite transfixed, while Mr Frees stands in the doorway, laughing. Presently he says, in his delightful, mellow voice, that if I am all that hungry, he has some food in his room next door – and so I follow him up there.

Mr Frees sits on a chair, making coffee in a battered saucepan, while I lie on the bearskin on his bed. We don't talk much, and presently – having duly fed me some cake – he goes out, saying I can stay there if I like. I lie awake all night waiting for him to come back, thinking that I have now fallen in love so deeply that it will surely last forever and that he of course will love me too.

He comes back as I am about to leave for my work. Where has he been all night? Well, with a woman of course. What did I suppose? He is amused, I am somewhat fractured. But I am willing to believe that, since it is he who has done this, it is somehow bound to be right.

I visit him a few more times like this. I find out his first name is 'Wolf', that he worked in the theatre in Berlin, is now working a bit for the BBC, that his wife is in the mental hospital at Shenley, and that he will come to see me in my room one night…

When he does come, I think I know well enough what will happen, and lie on my bed waiting, thinking this is bound to be exciting and pleasant or people would not keep doing it.

Since my childhood in Switzerland, I have been so ashamed of my useless, painful body that about the worst thing I could think of at all would be for anyone to see it naked. So what did I think was going to happen?

Mr Frees stands by my bed, laughing, undresses me completely, and then makes love to me with considerable, painful, violence. I lie there completely paralysed, staring at his two black eyes, which stare back, laughingly. Presently he disappears onto the floor at the foot of the bed and starts up doing something altogether different. Now I think I am going to fall to pieces altogether, break my back at the very least… Thirty years later, I shall be told that my physical reactions to this event are unusual, to say the least. This may well account for some aspects of my future.

Presently Mr Frees is sitting on my bed again. I say something (an expression of total astonishment, I think) that causes him to laugh and laugh even more. Soon he starts up to do the whole thing all over again. What did I think of all this? I really don't know, except that I was glad to be so clearly entertaining to Mr Frees. I think he will now be sure to stay with me forever. In fact, he does not. He has many women he likes to spend his nights with and, after explaining this, does not come often to my room for a month or two.

At the Medical Research Institute, I am getting very worried by the number of bodies of mice that I have to dispose of. I see that it is 'mental' to keep on killing off these pretty little creatures (they are Argentine mice, not like ordinary ones) but I simply cannot stop. One day, I take off my overall, tell the other girl on this floor that I am leaving and take off without even collecting my pay.

I stay in the house now for a few days, either alone in my room or with the other people here, who are mostly refugees and so have learned the hard way never to ask questions. Presently, my wits somewhat restored, I look in the paper for another job.

Mr Reik, in Soho, wants an 'experienced hand-weaver', which sounds all right to me, being still manual labour. Mr Reik is in Poland Street, where he has a dusty room full of looms operated by Czech women. They are making fancy scarves (now much in fashion) for the Liberty store. I have never seen a loom before but persuade Mr Reik to let me try, unpaid for two weeks, since I see that I can do it – have to, anyway.

After one week, I can do it as well as anyone else here (they are enraged – Mr Reik is pleased and astonished) and so I stay here for about a year. We work from 8 to 6, with half an hour off for lunch. Since it is 'piece work', I do it as fast as possible in order to earn £5 a week.

In fact, it is very exhausting work indeed, but soon my arms and legs move automatically and leave me free to think other things. After about six months, Mr Reik makes me 'overseer' and I design all the materials instead of making them. The Czechs are very hostile indeed about this but all I care about is making £5 a week.

At Kingswell House now, something happens that I am going to feel terrible about for the rest of my life. My sister Felicity, working in a factory somewhere, phones me to ask if she can borrow my room for one night, with a man who works with her. My sister with a man? I really don't believe this but say of course she can, since I can stay with Wolf.

My sister has always said she is going to marry a bishop, but what turns up with her now is clearly a very nasty piece of work altogether, called Leslie. He will remain so after becoming my brother-in-law. Leslie was a corporal in the army for 20 years until a bridge fell on him. He once molested my daughter, Antonia, and has been found in bed with the maid, etc, etc.

Leslie, large, dark and sullen, wants to go straight to the pub next door, although I see he's had enough already. He sits there by the fire and orders me to go out and get drinks. Now that I am used to Continental manners, I am outraged by this uncouth creature. I take his money and buy everything I can think of: bring it all to him on a tray and watch him drink the lot.

Next morning, looking to see if they have left my room, I see Felicity lying naked on the bed, while Leslie is naked and senseless on the floor. The room looks as if it has been hit by a bomb. I pour a bottle of peroxide over Leslie's black hair and go off to work, hoping that is the last I shall see of him.

At about this time, a very pleasant young man downstairs asks me to his room. He is a medical student, about to go into the Navy as a surgeon. He is very worried because, having seen so many bodies both dead and alive and usually unpleasant, he finds himself unable to sleep with a woman at all. So would I mind? I am sorry for poor, handsome Adam, and since Wolf has other women too, I say of course, do what you like. But it is not any use after all and he goes off to war unhappy, to be blown up at once.

I have been at Kingswell House for some time now and one Sunday morning Wolf and I are discovered asleep together in bed. Miss Beatty is very nice and very sorry, but this really will not do at all and we must both go as soon as possible, when we find somewhere to go.

I know that if I am to stay with Wolf, I must now find two rooms for almost nothing and with no landlady to throw us out. I knock on many, many doors and come at last to what I want, in Belsize Park. This is a very tall, grey house, owned by a very small, grey, Chinese woman who only comes round once a month to collect the rents.

There are about 50 assorted refugees here, one toilet in the basement, one bath a bit further up and one other which is clearly used as a toilet as well. There are two attics, connected by a catwalk, at the very top. They have yellow, peeling walls, many maggots living in the greasy remains of carpet round the gas rings, nothing much in the way of furniture - but here we shall be left alone and it will do well enough. Wolf, being almost penniless, and still amused by me, agrees to come: and so my life with him, among the refugees, will start.

Chapter Five

I am just 18 when one afternoon my sailor boy turns up, almost unrecognisable, straight from some dreadful battle.

He is in a truly awful state, his uniform in tatters, he is black from head to foot. I run across the catwalk to ask Wolf what to do. He says to give this young man whatever he may want until the morning. Then I must explain my situation and send him off for good.

I put my Johnny – something of a hero, he was – into the bath, scrub him all over, do the best I can about his uniform and so to bed with him, for the first and last time ever. In the morning I explain, and watch him go off for good without a single word except goodbye. He takes one aspect of my life away with him and leaves a sort of pain and guilt that will repeat itself so many times in years to come...

One day Wolf comes home with a suit that he has bought from another refugee. To explain this miracle, he tells me that he now has full-time work with the US Army Broadcasting Service in Europe, or ABSIE, which has a secret broadcasting station somewhere in Soho.

This is very good news, as we are very cold and hungry. I can now stop picking the lock on the gas meter and Wolf comes to meet me in Poland Street most mornings for a meal of hot soup.

At nights I wait until one o' clock when a staff car brings Wolf home to continue my education in bed. He comes into the room, kisses my hand and takes all the clothes off us both immediately. He tells me exactly what the girls do in the brothels of Berlin and shows me how to do the same, within the limitations of our room.

Wolf really does enjoy this very much indeed and finds my ignorance a constant entertainment – only an English girl could be so ignorant! During these nights and all the nights and 'times off' for the next few years, I learn that, in order to show true love for Wolf, I must agree, for instance, to pass water into his mouth while giving him orgasms with my mouth at the same time. I must always, several times each night, swallow all the results of Wolf's orgasms and if I try to spit it out I am told this means that I do not truly love him – that I am failing to 'give myself' properly. The same applies if I protest that

43

I have my period: apart from pain, what about the mess? But no. I am quite wrong, this is actually the best time of the month to show my love for him. Well, I learn, and Wolf is very pleased.

I am relieved that there are no suitable animals, hunchbacks, whips or so on available for extra entertainment in this room. In fact, for all I know, Wolf is a perfectly reasonable man. I do try very hard to believe this and to look forward to the car door slamming outside at one o'clock.

My basic problems here are that, after a long and hard day's work, I am physically exhausted long before one o'clock, and three hours' sleep is simply not enough. I am soon too tired to make a real orgasm myself and so learn to pretend, which leaves me nervous and unable to sleep easily at all.

At six o'clock I must get up and try to clean myself up well enough, which is very difficult here indeed, to start the long journey into Soho, to my work.

Worse, I simply cannot make any sense at all out of the two totally different aspects of Wolf's personality. In the daytime, he shows me every possible consideration and respect. He deprives himself to bring me presents: brings me books to read, which open worlds and visions I had hardly dreamt of; brings me to his friends, with whom I am enchanted. I find them all very interesting to listen to, very charming, very amusing and very, very kind. They are mostly Jews (they call themselves the Enemy Alien Refugees from Nazi Oppression), which Wolf is not.

They almost all treat him with admiration and respect, in spite of his sarcastic manner with them. I ask Wolf if he has something against Jews – after all, he married one? He says they are clever enough but will insist on suffering all the time, no matter what.

Wolf had a Prussian father, so I suppose that accounts for his attitude and general arrogance. Of course his name is not 'Wolf Frees' at all. When the war is safely over, he admits to being a top Nazi's nephew, which may well explain how he got himself out of Germany with his wife as late as he did.

Wolf has been to see Dr Lambert, who remembers him from the theatre in Berlin. Wolf comes back laughing and tells me Lambert is a phony. What do I think an Austrian Jew is doing, playing psychiatrist in London with a very English-sounding name?

But Lambert clearly is making a success of it, so that is all right. In fact, I can see that Wolf has quite approved of Lambert, but even if he does not, I am not concerned about anything to do with Lambert except that he shall stay put and be exactly the same, phony or not.

One morning I leave Mr Reik's little factory for my half-hour lunch and walk towards Oxford Street, to see if Wolf is coming to meet me. At the corner, I stop in my tracks to watch a great, big, black, V-1 flying bomb skimming the roofs opposite, apparently about to land exactly on my head. I register that, since its engine must have cut out some time ago, there is simply nothing I can do but stand and wait…

Presently I wake up pressed against a wall in Oxford Street. Lying in the road nearby is a milkman's horse with its head lying beside it and very great deal of blood spouting out of its neck. Further down, some building is collapsing very slowly, without making a sound at all. There is a thick fog of dust all over everything.

Finding myself still intact but very dirty, I run to the Corner House where there are public washrooms. There is more commotion here, because a lift full of people has fallen and those who may still be alive cannot get out.

Running back to Poland Street, slightly cleaned up, I find I cannot see what I am doing. Mr Reik, though distant, has never shown any ill will to me and so I go to him and try to explain that, although I am unhurt, I simply can't stop crying. Mr Reik stares a bit and says OK, better go home, since I clearly cannot work anymore today.

I do not go home, but run straight across Soho to Mayfair. Dr Lambert's waiting room is clearly not for me in this condition, so I sit on the floor outside his room, hoping he is there or may turn up some time.

Presently I can hear Lambert talking German, apparently to me. I am comfortable, lying down, looking at the big blue painting on the wall. Lambert is telling me to go to sleep, but I protest – there is something I want to explain. Perhaps I finally want to explain why it is I can't sleep much these days.

I hear him say I am going to sleep now for two weeks at least, which sounds so crazy that I give up protesting, feel the weight of his big white hand covering my eyes and remember absolutely nothing more from this moment until at least two weeks later.

I wake up in a strange room – large and white, with a white, wooden ceiling. Looking around, I see Felicity in a bed nearby, sitting up with her arms around her knees, staring out of the window at the sea, tears streaming down her face. Every single aspect of this scene is so absolutely unexpected that I am completely wide awake at once and sit up too.

My sister tells me that we are in a hotel at Lyme Regis, where I have been kept asleep for the past two weeks. Mama is here too. My sister is crying because she is going to have a baby. Why cry, then? Hasn't she always wanted babies?

Oh no, not Leslie! Yes indeed and she does not think he will marry her. She cannot possibly have an illegitimate child - what will Parents say? What on earth can she do?

I remember the tray full of drinks I so foolishly caused Leslie to drink and know that my poor sister's life is messed up forever – through my fault again. It is too. Mama does not want an illegitimate child in the family, Papa virtually disowns her – and life with Leslie is one long, total misery.

Back in Belsize Park with Wolf, I find that my paternal grandmother has gone mad in some remote village in Scotland, given her fortune to a young man in the village post office and finally died. The young man gave grandma's money back to her companion and a few hundred pounds are now coming to me. Not much, but I reckon I can live without working for a year or so and do what I like instead.

Wolf and I decide that St Martin's School of Art is where I can best set out to be a painter. I go there to be duly interviewed, accepted and told to start off with Life Drawing and Sculpture.

Arriving at 10am on my first day with paper, drawing board, charcoal and a feeling of utter panic, I look down a long, empty corridor for somewhere to be sick. There are little drinking fountains all down the wall and one of these will have to do.

By now I am late. I open a studio door to see a plumcoloured, naked woman standing quite transfixed on a platform in front of about 30 students who are drawing her. They are silent, totally absorbed. At the back of the room is a big man with a red beard and a wooden leg – our instructor, Ruskin Spear, fast asleep.

No one even turns to look at me. I sit and start to draw here in this quiet room where I am going to be very happy indeed for a year or two at least. We draw from 10 until one and again from two until four every weekday. Sometimes I go to the Sculpture Studio to copy various bits of David's anatomy in clay.

I can now get a reasonable amount of sleep (my Seconals can work themselves off in peace) and Wolf fetches me for a proper lunch most days. After school, I sometimes go to the cinema, which pleasure has been forbidden since Dr Statham said it was bad for me, way back in some other life. Wolf and I go to see the Continental films that we both enjoy.

At home in the evenings, I enjoy the books Wolf brings me, and my drawings, which he admires tremendously. I make a little clay model of an old monk with a dog. I enjoy every moment of these days so much, but I am still utterly confounded at one o'clock, which brings an hour or two of sickening confusion every night.

One day, in the Sculpture Studio, I watch a soldier trying to make his difficulties over David's foot understood to his instructor in a language that I recognise but do not understand, Polish. Mr Maraden looks bemused, the soldier despairs and I try interpreting in very basic French. Success. The soldier is delighted, clicks his heels, kisses my hand and declares himself to be Count D'Arbogast Prozyniski, or Conrad, if it will please you to call him so.

We are friends at once and for evermore (he turns up in Durban many years later). At last, a totally uncomplicated, unconditional, always pleasant, relationship. I may wonder what a perfectly healthy, young-ish Pole in a brand new, absolutely anonymous army uniform is doing at this art school. All the other students are either too young for service or excluded as unfit C3s such as me. But one does not ask such things. In fact, I never did ask him anything about himself at all.

After school, we ride around London on Conrad's bicycle, ending up usually at his room in Bayswater. This room is very small and clean – it has a packing case, a radio, a heavily-embroidered Polish rug. Nothing else at all.

Conrad lays his overcoat on the rug on the floor and makes love to me with a simple tenderness and consideration that causes me further

47

mental somersaults because I find myself enjoying all this very much indeed. Conrad does not want to show me what goes on in the brothels of Warsaw and probably would be a little shocked to find I know anyway. Quite often we lie on the overcoat, under the rug, and simply doze or talk a bit, content to lie there in each other's arms.

Sometimes a very splendid Polish officer comes in and Conrad has to go out in a hurry. Sometimes we go to the Polish Eagle Club next door, where he disappears for a while.

Mostly we just stay in the room and talk, make love, listen to the radio, sleep. Presently I wish I do not always have to get up and make the long journey back to Belsize Park by one o'clock. I ask Wolf if I can please stay out with Conrad all night, sometimes at least. Wolf says all Poles are absolutely ridiculous but I had better bring this one to see him since I am evidently hell-bent on being ridiculous as well.

Wolf sits on a straight-backed chair in our room. Conrad lies on his back on the floor. I sit on the bed and listen to them talking on and on in German, half the night it seems. Wolf looks very amused and presently tells me that out of the whole preposterous Polish nation my friend is quite surely the very most absurd of all. And so? I really don't remember if I ever went again to Conrad's room, although I know I missed it very much and he of course remained my friend.

Wolf meanwhile has a very bright idea indeed… He tells me to meet him in the early evening somewhere in Soho. He takes me to a very dilapidated door on a very dilapidated house, down one of the back streets. Down some wooden steps, inside, I see a rather grubby Sidney Greenstreet sort of character sitting in a dim light by a little switchboard.

It seems we are expected, and through another dilapidated door I find myself in all the luxury and comfort provided by the American Army for its European broadcasting service. Wolf takes me along a few miles of corridors to the canteen, brings me a tray of food such I have not seen for years, brings a very stern-looking Hungarian friend of his called Julius to keep me company at his table, and goes off to the studios to get on with his work.

Later on that night, Wolf comes back with the CO, Colonel Hannan, who is big, blond and very nice indeed. He talks to me for a bit and talks in German to Wolf. He presently decides I am not any sort of risk for the American Army. In fact, I can come here every night that Wolf is here, provided I stay in the canteen. A staff car will take us home together at one o'clock…

ABSIE is an irresistibly exciting place to me and I go there just as often as I can – bombs, work and sleep permitting. A soldier takes me down to the canteen and there I sit and talk to Wolf or to one of his friends who will be there to keep me company.

My favourite companion here is Golo Mann, whose job it is to write out instant retaliations to Dr Goebbel's Nazi propaganda. Golo looks like an enraged black bull. He is absolutely fed up with being the famous author Thomas Mann's son, fed up with the unspeakable 'Dr Gobbles', loves Wolf most dearly – and cannot ever, ever sleep. I share my Seconals and Benzedrines with him and get some extra ones from Dr Lambert, who, I think, takes over Golo's problems too.

I really am convinced that Wolf does truly love me very much. He tells me that a woman must be loved, and looked after, and made a fuss over, all the time. That is what they need and want and ought to have. Of course, I agree entirely with these views and see that Wolf is living up to them very well as far as I am concerned, most of the time anyway.

He tells me that when his wife has been certified insane for long enough they can be divorced (without her knowing) and then he will marry me. When he tried to divorce her before, she first jumped into the pond at Shenley Asylum and then cut the sleeves of her coat and tried to hang herself with them. I have not seen her yet. Wolf says she is just a poor little animal now and will never be able to leave Shenley. When the war is over, he will take me to see her…

It is late 1944 and I suddenly find myself absolutely petrified of the war. I think I may be killed after all by the latest secret weapon thought up by the opposition. The V-2 rocket cannot be seen or heard arriving – it simply lands with the most appalling crash, no warning whatsoever, seemingly at random. Our ancient house shakes and rocks and shudders. Up in my attic, I seriously consider trying to evade this monster by going to the Underground. But time goes by and we – and even the house – survive this too.

At ABSIE, there is even more excitement than usual – the news machines are going at terrific speed and the soldiers talk of home.

Near St Martin's School of Art, young schoolboys, who are going to miss fighting in the war altogether, drop French Letters full of Indian ink on passersby in Charing Cross Road to relieve their feelings. Even Ruskin Spear is seen to wake up and watch them, and the models have some trouble keeping still.

One day I watch a flying bomb passing over London and wonder if that is the last one I shall see. In fact it is. Wolf, listening to the news, says that the war, for us, is over. Don't I want to go down into the city and watch all the excitement? No. I stay in my room until the celebrations are over.

Excitement that night? No. For me, the end of this war seems to mean nothing much at all and I stay in my room until the celebrations are over.

I look for somewhere else for Wolf and I to live and find a one-roomed flat in Swiss Cottage, which is a district for refugees. Our landlord here is Herbert Palmer. I see him for the first time while he is shovelling up horse manure (for his garden) in the road outside his house.

Old Palmer is very tall, very gaunt, with a lot of wild, unwashed hair, a white beard, two or three teeth and a black velvet jacket. Having a shot at respectability, I say I want to live here with my 'guardian'. Old Palmer says, with surprising kindness, don't be silly. He doesn't care who I live with as long as one of us pays the rent.

Our flat is small and dirty but at least it's 'self-contained'. I learn to cook a bit when the gas is on and food is available (all very scarce in England at this time). I enjoy having a proper bath, except that Wolf is now able to show me exactly what can be done in a bath together, under water.

Old Palmer lives in a big room by the front door, piled up to the roof with dusty furniture and books. I find out by chance, from an anthology, that he is a famous poet.

But, reading his gentle verses, I am astonished by his wild behaviour to his wife. This poor lady, who actually owns the house, turns up from time to time but never gets far inside the front door. Old Palmer simply roars at her and throws her violently down the front steps every time.

Eventually, long after I have gone, I hear that he has done this once too often, breaking her bones, and has died in the hospital of Brixton jail where he has been kept for contempt of court, refusing flatly to say he is sorry about anything at all. Well, he was to be a very good friend to me…

One evening, Wolf brings Colonel Hannan to our flat and they sit beside the fire talking in German, clearly making plans about the future. I sit on the floor, with my head on Hannan's lap while he strokes my hair. 'This is an original,' he says to Wolf. Much gratified by this remark, I consider that 'all the others' are not to be envied as people living better lives than I.

We go out to eat at the Cosmo (Wolf knows Mr Cosmo from Berlin) and here I watch the actress Beatrix Lehmann at the next table with her latest little-girl waif, which is such an ugly scene I cannot describe it here.

Wolf tells me now that he is going off to Europe to look for his relatives. His friend, Dr Jacobi in Lincolns Inn, makes arrangements for my future in case he does not get back again. Wolf puts on an American soldier's uniform, reminds me not to answer questions and gives me a record of himself reading some of my favourite verses from Rilke.

He says he will phone from Paris and from Hamburg if he gets that far. As he goes, my world collapses and I feel that I shall die of grief.

I take my call from Paris in old Palmer's room one night. Afterwards, to cheer me up, he plays Wagner on his gramophone, full blast, while he roars over it, explaining the story as it goes along. Our friendship is consolidated by the gift of a large piece of coal that I find in my mailbox the next morning.

The call from Hamburg comes as well. More tears, more Wagner, and next morning I see old Palmer fall flat on his face in the garden. I help him crawl back into his room and run for our brandy – just a little stroke, he says, and brandy should do the trick. We finish it off together. Perhaps it was about this time that I started on the downward path to drink.

During the weeks Wolf is away, I do not go out much but roam around my room listening to the gramophone, hoping for some message that I know I can't expect to come. Conrad visits me sometimes and we draw each other. Wolf's friends visit me sometimes and ask for news. The feeling I have, remembering this time, is of fear, darkness and confusion, followed by a new intensity about my work. I have a new belief that I am, really am, one day going to be a painter and that will be the most important thing about my life.

One evening, after about three weeks, the door opens and Wolf comes in, still in uniform, looking like a ghost.

He sits by the fire in his overcoat, staring, saying nothing, unable to come back to life at all. In fact, it is quite a few days before he does begin to tell me something of what he has seen in his journey across Europe and back.

His mother and other relatives are safe in Lubeck. Every month now, we send them a big parcel of food and clothing, such as we can get.

Wolf goes to work at the BBC and I go back to school. I start to paint now at St Martin's, and then draw at the Central School until 10 at night. Wolf and I eat at the Cosmo often, since there is very little food in the shops. In fact, London at this time is very battered and gloomy indeed. You have to queue up for one piece of bread, which you may or may not get.

On Sundays sometimes we take the train to Shenley, where Wolf's wife stands at the gate to meet us, barefoot in the snow, wearing many strange and sleeveless clothes all on top of each other. She seems to like me very much and we take her for tea or else sit in the ward with her. She looks terrible and very sad. She appears to understand nothing at all except that Wolf, her love, is here. I go to Shenley only a few times, since I cannot really bear this tragic situation so close up.

Quite often I visit my father, who is no longer working in the Christadelphian Hall with Litzi but looking after thousands of wild refugees from Malta on Putney Heath. Litzi has married somebody called Horace but dies shortly afterwards.

Sometimes I go to spend a night with Mama, who has a horrid little house in Seaford, on the coast. Next door lives her friend Phyl, although she spends most of the time with Mama. This woman has nicotine stains all around her mouth from the cigarette that is a permanent fixture. She has a raucous voice, frightful cough and plays the radio all the time so loud I think it, or I, will fall to pieces. Her relationship with Mama is most painfully apparent and I come here as seldom as possible.

At home in London, life is getting very difficult. It seems to me that I love Wolf more and more each day, but his increasing demands upon my body have now become so repellent that I simply don't know how to bear it.

I cannot hide my feelings either, so Wolf and I are both distraught. I see him standing naked by the bed, beseeching me to love his body, and I close my eyes, give up pretending since it is beyond me, and simply try to fade out of this, hope he will just one day understand, and stop...

I have been for some years very friendly with Wolf's girlfriend Patricia, who, since she can't have Wolf, is about to marry a writer who is to become an author of note, John Berger. She is in fact the girl Wolf spent the night with the first time he and I met. Well now, if this lovely girl can enjoy Wolf's love-making as much as they both say she does, then why can't I? I just don't know – and feel myself falling to pieces in despair.

Dr Lambert, brooding one evening over such of my problems as I may have been able to explain, says if I will put on a dress he will take me dancing at the Ritz. Well, I do not possess a dress and could not dance to save my life, so I clearly have not explained much at all well and simply burst into tears all over again.

Lambert thinks again and says if I come on a certain evening I shall find someone I shall like very much indeed in the waiting room. I find a truly beautiful Bavarian painter called Jupp, who has a wife about 20 years older than himself and a young daughter. Well, Lambert certainly was trying hard to tidy our lives up a bit for us, but Jupp and I are too far sunk to even enjoy each other's company much and soon give up trying.

Lambert, my most constant comfort over the years, is going to America now, to see about punch-drunk boxers there. He tells me that my life will never be an easy matter and it is no use trying to escape this fact.

He tells Papa that only a 'profound Freudian analysis' is likely to be much lasting help – and he gives me the address of Dr Westman, whom I ought to go to now. I don't want to see any other doctor and will not go (but fortunately keep the address). I cannot bring myself to say goodbye to Dr Lambert, even on the telephone.

Mama writes that she and Phyl are going to stay in our old home in Switzerland for a few weeks. Would I like to come too and bring a friend? I remember Rachel, whom I quite liked long ago in Kingswell

House, and the four of us set off together in an aeroplane. In the little wooden train winding up through the mountains to Chateau D'Oex, I feel tremendously excited. Wolf, after waving goodbye at the airport, fades a bit. I choose a room I never slept in before in my old home.

It is summer, and all very beautiful and peaceful here. Nothing really seems to have changed in all these years – except of course for Mama and Phyl behaving even more blatantly than usual all over the house. Rachel bears it silently, reading Latin in the kitchen, and then she says she is going home at once.

Looking around for company in the village bistro, I find myself an Alpine Guide who wants to show me 'how they do it in Switzerland'. This takes place on a rocky mountainside and is every bit as unsatisfactory as one might expect.

I cross the river and climb as far up the other side as I can get, I sit on my balcony and try to paint, I write every day to Wolf and, in a sense, enjoy this holiday quite well enough.

Back in Swiss Cottage, very far from Switzerland, life goes on getting worse and worse as Wolf and I get more and more unhappy. Presently Mama writes again. She does not wish to die at the sink in Seaford – she wants to go and live in South Africa with Phyl, who is already in Cape Town.

But Mama does not feel able to go so far away and leave me behind, clearly in a bad way. Papa writes that I must make up my own mind about this, but he has also noticed my bad state and feels South Africa would be best for everybody. But they will certainly not be able to go unless I agree to come too, on any terms whatever that I might suggest. Papa has sold up and is positively loaded all over again.

I don't know how long it takes for me to decide, but only that I answer that I will come just for one year and must be housed at all times quite apart from them so I can lead my own life. I do not propose to exchange suffocation by Wolf for suffocation by Mama, which might be worse, as I remember it.

Wolf says South Africa is absolutely the most absurd place in the whole world. With hazy visions of covered wagons in the desert alternating with steaming jungles full of hostile savages, I quite agree. I tell Wolf one year is not so long and I can't very well say no anyway, can I?

Presently he sees I really mean to go and brings his friends around to reason with me. Jacobi, Patricia, John, Julius, Schaffer, Norbert – they all say one way or another that Wolf will break his heart if I do go and I shall simply be ruining his life.

Elizabeth Ligeti, the only one who always did answer Wolf back, says she sees my problems but I should consider that no one else will ever in my life love me as Wolf does. He is the most remarkable man, as I must surely know.

Oh yes, I do know very well, but of course can't explain to anyone at all just why it is I really have to go. So I just listen, and watch them all getting to hate me for my selfish, wilful, stupidity.

I say goodbye to Wolf in our flat and take a taxi to the KLM airline office in Sloane Street. Jacobi arrives here and tries very hard to persuade me not to go. As the airport bus leaves the terminal, I see Wolf jump out of a taxi waving his arms and calling out.

I remember this very clearly now, but nothing else until our plane is coming down to land at Amsterdam. Here I notice the very handsome, charming little boy who is sitting beside me – my brother Julian, in fact, now 11 years old and very excited by this journey.

An early photogragh of Hilary
taken by her father, Roger Carter

Hilary with her older sister, Felicity
(on the right)

Hilary on her bed chair doing lessons

Chateaux d'Oex, Switzerland

Left: John 'Johnny' Crawford-Kennedy

Above: Hilary sculpting David's foot at St Martin's School of Art

Above: Count Conrad D'Arbogast-Prozyniski

Hilary with her brother, Julian 'Quag'

From left: Eileen Carter, Hilary, Roger Carter, Felicity and Vere

From left: Back row – Jane Grant, Felicity, Timothy, Hilary, Julian and Eileen
Front row – Leslie Grant, Susan Grant, Roger

David Furneaux

Vere Holden-White

Wolf Frees

John Kevan, in the doorway of Hilary's rondawel

Wendy Beckwith

John Kevan (with Hilary's dog Max)

Hilary

Hilary and Timothy Ramsden

Chapter Six

August 1947 – Amsterdam is a sea of bicycles, some lovely old buildings beside the canals and huge, ornate barrel organs everywhere. I remember a young girl in the hotel (a friend of Papa), showing me her abdomen which has big, swollen ridges, which look very painful. She is in great distress because it seems this condition cannot be cured.

We stay here about three days. I take Julian to see 'The Hunchback of Notre Dame', after which he goes about all screwed up pretending to be the hunchback and being so funny I call him 'Quag' hereafter. Still do.

We fly over the desert in the moonlight (so beautiful I wish it would just go on forever) to land briefly at Tripoli. Then a stop at Kano, which is hot and dusty, with vultures sitting about everywhere. At Leopoldville, we actually spend a night in bed. The surroundings are suitably African, with black people lying about in striped blankets and a little elephant chained to a stump nearby.

Finally we arrive at Johannesburg, which is quite the most hideous place I have ever seen in my life. We are met and entertained by Mr Gundlefinger (now called Gundle as he says he thought it diplomatic to lose the finger during the war), who is the agent here for Papa's family business.

There are many letters from Wolf for me at the hotel and I spend most of the time writing back. All our letters are more or less unrelieved anguish.

Mr Gundle takes us to buy a big, blue, Hudson motor car, which Papa drives very slowly on the wrong side of the road all the way to Cape Town. Mama, Julian and I go by train (why?) as far as Bloemfontein, where I am so ill that we stop for a day or two until Papa catches up and we proceed with him in the car.

In the hotel at Bloemfontein, I somehow acquire an admirer called de Villiers, private secretary to the Minister of Health. He later tracks me down in Durban, so I suppose I must have communicated with him.

All I remember of our onward journey to Cape Town is stopping at some horrible little village to buy brandy for Papa, who is feeling ill. There are only men in the bar, where I sit down to have a drink myself. They stare and laugh, and presently the barman says girls are not allowed in here, but he will sell me a bottle to take away.

In Cape Town, where Parents intend to settle, we stay in a guest farm, which is utterly horrible. There is a beastly old Ouma, who is making soap out of donkeys and actually proud of it. We all hate Cape Town and I am completely unnerved by the big, grey mountain with its top half cut clean off, which you simply cannot get away from.

We look at pictures of Durban, which is said to be warmer and appears more inviting than this cold, wet, windy place. We and the car are loaded onto a boat as quickly as possible and set off up the coast.

In the barroom of the Cape Town Castle, I acquire a very nice-looking, amusing young Englishman called David Furneaux. He is a former RAF Wing Commander, on his way to Durban to look for a nice, comfortable life. He is very lively – exactly the reverse of all I have been used to up to now. Furneaux and I spend this voyage drinking in the bar, or – when I am not occupied with writing to Wolf – fornicating in his cabin. He has no particular sexual habits but simply an unprecedented enthusiasm for this activity. I proceed, very hot, very drunk, and glad to be laughing at Furneaux's endless jokes and capers, all the way to Durban.

Parents are very pleased with Furneaux and also with Durban when we get there. We all stay together in various hotels while Papa looks for a house.

I continue hot and drunk in bed with Furneaux most of the time but am also learning how to drive a car. I wreck two before I can do this, more or less. Papa gives me a pretty little open car, which I drive always as fast as it will go, scaring myself witless and presumably enjoying this.

Now Papa has a very nice house in Westville and has built for me a charming cottage in the garden. We have six servants, three cars and anything else it may occur to anyone to want.

Furneaux has a flat in Durban where we spend the evenings, hot and drunk on the bed after a usual session at the yacht club. Wishing to harmonise with my new surroundings, I grow my hair long and take to wearing dresses and much jewellery, thus removing one part of myself as far as possible from the other part, which has stayed behind with Wolf in London.

Having always rather disliked animals, I now ask for a dog – and get the most expensive and beautiful alsation that can be found. I call him Max, grow very fond of him, and he is with me always, wherever I go in Africa, until he dies of old age many years later.

One morning I find my father, down by the river at the bottom of the garden, and I ask him what he truly thinks of Furneaux. He is embarrassed, laughs a bit, and says – well, a good chap of course, but don't you think perhaps just a little bit fatuous? I agree that this is clearly so and retire to my studio to consider the empty easel, empty walls, empty bottles, empty, fatuous days and nights just going on and on.

Back in Furneaux's bedroom I tell him I am not happy because I want to paint – and to get started I need other painters to talk to. He says that's easy, he knows just the right man, a 'wizard type' he has met at the yacht club and will 'wheel round' at once. So, from Furneaux's balcony, I watch John Kevan walking up the road to join us and to talk to me about painting.

John is very big, and blond, and handsome. He is suitably covered with paint and looks to me not only the most beautiful but also the most 'solid' sort of person I have ever come across. We do not talk about painting that evening, but sit and look at each other silently, enjoying the prospect of our future together.

When it is time for Furneaux to take me home, I ask John if he will come too and stay with me, since this was a foregone conclusion the moment he came into the room and neither of us could really bear to wait. Furneaux is astounded, tries not to appear upset and drives us home, where John and I spend a very happy, perfectly platonic night in my bed.

At breakfast, I introduce John to my parents, explain that he is coming to live with me and we are now going to collect his belongings from the derelict tug in the harbour where he has been staying. John and I set off with my dog Max for the yacht club, where John keeps a little dinghy. We sail in it across the harbour to the remains of the tug. Here in the cabin, we drink some wine, make love together in the sun with much delight, and I feel truly safe and very, very happy. Well, most of me does at this moment, anyway.

At home now, John hangs up his paintings in my studio, puts his easel next to mine and puts away the only other possessions he has, which are a few clothes, a big Luger pistol and a commando knife that he carries with him always, even when swimming in the sea. He was a commando in the desert during the war and I know that he has killed many people with this knife, though he does not like to talk about this much. The only time I saw him angry was when I once picked up his gun.

I don't know if he has any relatives, but he does have a child and a wife – he is in the middle of being divorced from her. They do not feature in my life.

John's main characteristic seems to be an unshakeable confidence in himself - he knows exactly what he wants, feels absolutely entitled to have whatever that may be and he knows he is going to get it. All of which I find very reassuring.

But we have something of a problem with Furneaux, who is lying on my bed incredibly in floods of tears. He says he cannot live without me and he will never love anyone else.

John tells me he knows a splendid girl, Michel Blake, whom he will bring around to meet Furneaux. Michel is an orphan, having a horrible time living with an uncle who does not want her. The four of us become very fond of each other indeed. Michel falls violently in love with Furneaux, but unfortunately he really did mean what he said about me.

When Furneaux comes from England to visit me in Umhlanga Rocks, north of Durban, many years later, he has a wife and children, is a senior executive with Marconi and spends much time floating round the world (often with John) in Mr Marconi's yacht. He appears to have the sort of life he wanted, but I find him to be a wreck of his former self. I hope I did not do this to him, but I rather think I did.

John and I have other friends as well now, mainly John and Helen Woods and the painter D'Oyly-John and his wife, Joan. We meet them by crashing into their car one day, whereupon they invite us back to their house nearby.

Here Joan leads John away, leaving me with D'Oyly-John sitting in his armchair in a dressing gown. He opens this to show me his naked body and we sit staring at each other across the room. Well, I like the look of him but do not propose to play games with him, so I just sit still and stare until he gets the message, gets dressed and shows me his pictures instead.

This is a very turbulent household – Joan and John throw food at each other and make a lot of noise, but I do not mind any of this and have no inclination to be 'unfaithful' to John with anyone at all at this time.

During these months, John and I spend our days painting or sailing about in the bay. Our evenings are spent with our various friends, either in my studio or on Salisbury Island, where we light a fire and lie about drinking most of the night. I love sailing around the bay at night and I think I am having fun with this life, as opposed to the rather heavy weather that has gone before.

But of course there are problems. I am physically unable to drink all round the clock with my companions without being sick, which happens violently every morning. My periods never turn up at the right time, which leads to general panic every month. Here I am saved by Dr Sandy Cuthbert, who is always a good friend to me and can be relied upon to get me out of trouble. He gets to understand me very well, and is surely the only doctor who could have produced my daughter Antonia for me all in one piece.

My Parents are not pleased with John. Papa because he beat the cook one day, Mama because he is destitute, has no intention of looking for work, and is perfectly content to ask for whatever he may need. She does, however, invite him to her bed – much to his amusement – but he will not agree to this and so she settles for D'Oyly, a fellow called Bill, Furneaux (after I have gone) and probably various others as well. She is being very social at this time, but keeps out of my studio and my life in general.

My worst problem is that I have continued to be split in two. Wolf and I write to each other most days: I tell him all about my present life, and tell John all about my past. John is understanding, sympathetic, kind. Wolf is amused, takes none of this seriously and writes

67

about my return when the year is up. As the time gets near, I get very upset indeed. I do not want to leave John – I love him and I want to stay with him, but I know that I belong to Wolf and should not break my promise to go back.

I am in tears much of this time now, cannot paint or enjoy anything much, feel very confused and ill. John says I must tell Wolf I am not going back but am staying here to marry him instead. He understands my dilemma but considers this the only possible thing to do and keeps on patiently explaining to me until at last I do write to Wolf and tell him exactly this.

After a few days, I get a cable back from Wolf, which has to be seen to be believed. It seems he has gone mad and injured himself somehow and all I can do now is get to him as quickly as possible.

There is a Dutch boat leaving for England the next day and Papa gets a double cabin on it for Michel and me. He pays her fare and gives her money so that she will look after me for the voyage at least. Fed up with her unrequited love for Furneaux, she is happy enough with this plan, while he moves in to cohabit with Mama.

John arranges to work his passage to England on another boat that is going the other way around and will arrive three weeks later than mine. He will then collect me in London, and by then Wolf must have been made to understand and accept this situation. I am aware that there is something fundamentally wrong with this whole arrangement, but I am in a panic and cannot see what else possibly can be done.

So, in September 1948, Michel and I – facing a somewhat uncertain future, with considerable alarm – set off in the Oranjefontein for England. We are closely followed by John, who is soon in trouble for sunbathing on the officers' deck when he ought to be washing up in the galley. But we are relying on him to rescue us from whatever disasters may be in store for us.

Chapter Seven

Soon after our ship leaves Durban, while in the cabin with Michel, I am seized suddenly with the most terrible pain I have ever had in my life.

I vomit all the time and scream uncontrollably until Michel brings me the ship's doctor, who takes one look at me and feeds me some big white pills, which he tells me later are pure opium. The pain goes away almost at once and does not come back here. I ask the doctor for more of these pills, since they have the effect of detaching me altogether from my body, but he will not give me any more and I feel he is viewing me with considerable disfavour.

In the bar, Michel and I feel that we are being looked upon with disfavour by just about everyone, so we take a bottle of brandy up to the deck, where I start to draw a comic-looking little man sitting in a deck chair. Presently he comes over to look at the drawing, introduces himself as Viscount Devonport and invites Michel and I for a drink before dinner.

Devonport is about 60, very pink (Michel and I call him 'the prawn') and clearly a collector of 'Bohemian Types' such as I appear to be. This is probably because his wife, Maria – young, glamorous and lately removed from being a model to become a diamond-dripping Lady Devonport – has taken to writing successful novels and needs to know as much as possible about different sorts of people.

Michel and I spend this voyage mostly with the Devonports, who are actually very pleasant people, and the entire crew treats us with great respect. I spend time with Maria, relating my fascinating life history – with enough alterations to make sure the result will be a bestseller.

Meanwhile Devonport is shut up with the Captain, telling him how to run his ship. So we proceed, hot and drunk (for my part anyway), all the way to Southampton, where Michel and I and the Devonports are now ready to expect absolutely anything.

As the ship comes in, I see Wolf in his long black overcoat and hat, standing apart from the general crowd, under a crane. Devonport has arranged the general difficulties of disembarking for me so that all I have to do is get off the ship and onto the boat train with Wolf.

I don't remember much of this except sitting in the restaurant car with Wolf, drinking as much as I can hope to keep down and trying to register as little as possible. Devonport comes down the car to have a look at this situation and promptly writes out his address for me, urging that I shall arrive at this ancestral home absolutely any time at all, if not at once. Michel has disappeared, heading for some distant relative in the country where she can stay while I arrange matters with F.

We arrive at a house in Sloane Street where Wolf has a flat on the top floor. At the last turning of the stairs there is a big banner pinned up with 'Welcome' painted on it, which causes me to understand at once, with total pain, exactly what situation I am really in.

Wolf shows me the flat – which is the sort most people in London want but can't get – and brings his friends Harold and Mirelle up to meet me from their flat downstairs. They are very nice, friendly, clearly devoted to Wolf and so happy for him that I am here. Mirelle is a Swiss girl, very big and very pregnant. Harold is a big, blond Scot. They are both young, only recently married and very much in love.

The next thing I remember is waking up in the morning looking at Wolf, who is lying in the bed with me asleep. He looks absolutely awful. His whole face is somehow changed, though I can't see any signs of injury and he has not appeared to be mad, or ill, or wounded. He looks incredibly old and dirty, most of his hair has fallen out and some of his teeth are missing. He smells awful, looks awful, and, after this moment of awful clarity, I black out again until evening.

We are in the living room now, in semi-darkness. Wolf is running about the room in his underpants, shouting and crying. The window is open and he presently jumps out of it and disappears. I run downstairs to Harold and Mirelle and collapse there on the floor, crying fit to die.

Presently I am aware that an ambulance has arrived. Later, I see Harold standing in front of me, looking terrible, saying that I have killed his baby. He says this over, and over, and over and I run back upstairs, find a big knife, and lock myself in the bathroom with it, lying on the floor. I stay there all day and night and maybe longer.

Now Harold has made me open the door and he stands there telling me that Mirelle has lost her baby because of the fright I gave her. She is in hospital. I don't know where Wolf is and I must get out of this house as quickly as I can.

I see that Harold would be glad to kill me right here and now and that is certainly what I deserve from every point of view. But he goes away and I lie on the bathroom floor with my knife and cry myself into oblivion. I think I stay like this for some days before I realise that I am not going to die – by knife or any other way. I can hear people moving about downstairs now, since my head is on the floor. I see that the sun is shining outside, remember John and Michel, and come slowly back to the idea of staying alive.

I remember trying to play the harpsichord in the living room and looking out of the window that Wolf jumped from, only to see that there is a flat roof of a big bay window just below, so Wolf could not possibly have hurt himself and maybe did not even intend to.

I must have sent a message to Michel at this time and remember wandering around Chelsea with her, looking for a room for us and another one for John when he arrives. We get a double one for us and a semi-basement, cabin-sized one for John in an old house packed with destitute artists, in Jubilee Place, off The Kings' Road.

Michel and I move into our room together, but presently I have to go every day to Sloane Street since John arrives at any time and will not know where to find me. I encounter Harold sometimes but he never speaks to me. I think a good deal happens here that I now cannot remember – there are friends of Wolf's about, and also Wolf himself, although he is not living here.

One day when I am sitting on the stairs hoping for the front doorbell to ring, it does, and there is John, big and brown, and solid as a rock as usual. My feelings and reactions at this moment need hardly be described, and presently we set off walking (nothing on earth could ruffle John enough to make him run), away from Sloane Street, down The Kings' Road, to the little room in Jubilee Place which is going to home for a little while at least.

Here John puts up an easel and spends most of his time painting pictures, which he hopes to sell. I spend my days with him or Michel, doing nothing in particular at all. I spend the nights with John, and sometimes Michel does too since she is lonely and in need of comfort too.

We take turns with the chair and the bed on occasions. We have financial problems now, since the money Papa sends me has to provide

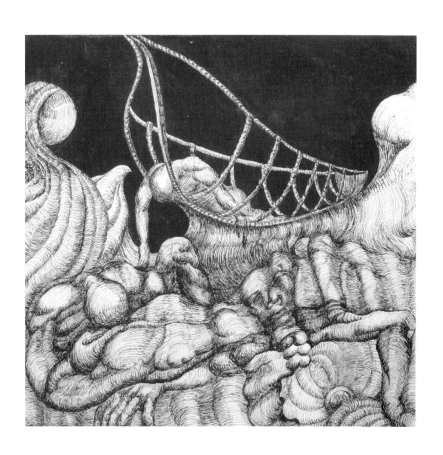

for all three of us. But John has a talent for 'acquiring' things, and most nights he cooks something for us and manages to bring milk and bread. He also washes all my clothes and me, since he is a very clean person and I don't seem to be able to look after myself properly at this time.

Presently I begin to wonder what did happen to Wolf while I was in Africa, and I go to look for Elizabeth, who is likely to know and be willing to explain to me. Elizabeth is a Hungarian actress, a refugee from Budapest, who looks as if everything that possibly could happen to someone has happened to her. She is kind and sensible.

She looks at idiotic me with pity and says that what happened was simply that Wolf got himself a facelift and a new nose, because he needed these for success as a film actor. The melodrama was simply because he knows me well enough to be sure that I will fall for it, rather than anything reasonable, and he was determined to get me back. She says he is mad, always was – that she warned me before I went, and that having gone I should have stayed as far away as possible.

Back in John's room I try to digest my truly disastrous behavior and stupidity, concluding that I must be mad as well and had better consult a psychiatrist before anything worse can happen. I remember the name that Dr Lambert gave me long ago and presently set off to see what Dr Westman can do about unscrambling the most confusing aspects of my life.

Dr Westman's room is grey, and dull, and uninviting. He is long and thin, with a black coat and homburg and a heavy German accent. He has a brown face, blue eyes, long white hair and an expression of permanent disapproval and bad temper. He has clearly settled for the 'objective' approach to psychiatric counselling and could hardly do otherwise, given his disposition. He could not hope to fool even a moron into believing that he actually liked them, even if he wanted to. However, he does look clever, and since I came here for advice rather than comfort, he may perhaps do well enough.

I see Dr Westman two or three times a week until the next time I leave this country. He favours the opinions of Dr Jung, who is a friend of his, rather than Freud (favoured by Dr Lambert) or Adler (favoured by Dr Statham). I write out everything I dream for him and try to explain the workings of my mind, rather than the problems of living my life.

I find that I can do what might be called 'automatic drawings', with my mind switched off from what I am doing, while my hand makes complicated (usually gruesome) pictures quite unlike any others which I like to do or can do.

Westman allows that these are interesting and says he will show them to his friend Jung in Switzerland. I sit in John's room in the evenings doing this whilst enjoying the company of other people amusing themselves in the room with us. I also write a short story like this once, but my hand stuck with some point towards the ending, which had then to be contrived and therefore was pointless.

After a few months in London, our collective financial position is getting desperate. Erik, one of the destitute painters upstairs, says he has met a very wealthy idiot who is looking for 'Bohemian' girls to show him the local colour, and since John has two of these available he should be well advised to see what we can do. Michel and I agree to this, and Erik comes downstairs with an Eastern European man who declares: 'Call me Bogo!'

He is large and white, with a round, white face, a great many gold teeth, grey hair, black homburg, camelhair coat and a general air of considerable (probably black market) riches. He looks just about as corny as anyone could be, but wastes no time removing Michel and I to his flat nearby. It is warm, luxurious, and he plies us with exotic food and drink, displaying all his gold teeth while he makes up his mind which of us is going to end up in his bed.

Reporting our evening to John, Michel says she simply does not feel up to it. Having noted Bogo's empty walls, I suggest that I can try to make him buy some of John's pictures and get away before the question of bed comes up.

So I spend more evenings alone with Bogo, being plied with food and drink in his flat. He buys me an awful dress, which I am obliged to wear. I extract three membership cards for the famous Pheasantry Club from Bogo and work on the question of John's pictures, while I wait for the moment when his fat, white paw is going to land on me.

One evening he greets me draped in a ludicrous 'scrambled-eggs-on-blood' type of dressing gown, leads me firmly to the bed and falls down flat on me like a big, white whale. This moment, which I should have been prepared for but was not, becomes positively alarming. Bogo weighs a ton, is very determined to get what he has been paying for, gives up trying to be charming and turns very nasty indeed. Only the peculiar strength of my hands gets me out of this (only just), and I am left with the conviction that rape is perfectly possible after all. I shall not try this sort of trick again.

John and I – drinking beer on Bogo's account at the Pheasantry – conclude that he will simply have to get a job and so he starts up painting scenery at Covent Garden, which he quite enjoys.

At this time I am getting very restive, unhappy, ill, confused. I get myself admitted to the Chelsea School of Art, where I turn up spasmodically to draw. I meet D'Oyly-John one day and spend the afternoon with him in John's bed. He and Joan have a house nearby and we visit them often – I talking to D'Oyly while he paints, while John is mostly with Joan, whose habits have not changed at all.

I visit Conrad, who has a vast, derelict studio not far away. He is as nice as ever, but does not make love with me any more since has a wife and child living behind a screen in the studio. He has just come out of Brixton jail and is now making decorations for tombstones here. He looks a mess – has lost most of his hair and teeth – but his inbuilt dignity and charm are just the same and he will recover soon. I spend a good deal of time with him and his wife, who is very nice though totally improbable in these surroundings.

All this time, Wolf is living in Chelsea too and I go and see him in his room from time to time. I do not remember anything about these meetings, but am fairly sure there is some sort of drama attached to them. I see him smiling, talking quietly and quite composed. I think I usually go to him for some sort of advice or other and he adopts a more or less fatherly attitude towards me.

I must have been showing my true feelings about myself very obviously, because one day Dr Westman loses his cool and his principle enough to snarl a more or less subjective remark at me. This is: 'Vy ze hell don't you just sometimes take a bath?' This gives me a considerable jolt and, after some advice from Wolf, I think, I go off to a very smart hairdresser in Sloane Square, from which I emerge with long, blonde, straight hair, draped over one eye, instead of a black, curly mat. I am absolutely delighted with this transformation, get some new clothes to go with it and take a quite unnecessary number of baths every day from now on.

If Westman is pleased about this, he does not say so. He is annoyed because I am not able to draw much for him now, explaining that the workings of my mind are more or less impossible, since it is usually a blank.

John has many friends at Covent Garden and one day says that Clement Golock - who is in charge of the painting there – is going to bring a 'brilliant' young painter round to see us. Clement is a splendid person and Michel and I entertain her while John cooks our supper and we wait for the brilliant young painter.

Presently there is an apparent waterfall from the street above and down into the area outside our room. John – much annoyed – says some man is relieving himself up there and splashing onto our window. Clement says that must be Vere and goes up to fetch him.

Vere is very tall and thin. He wears an awful suit that is much too small for him, held up with red braces. He is dirty, smelly, noisy, rude, in very high spirits and – to me – absolutely fascinating. He has truly brilliant blue eyes and brilliant (though often obscene and usually insulting) conversation.

The terrific impact of his personality knocks me clean out of my stupor and I hope sincerely (though he is distinctly terrifying) that I shall see him again. John thinks he is absolutely the most bitter end and poor Michel is in too bad a state to have noticed much at all.

She has recently had some disaster that led her to be confronted by a whole group of psychiatrists in a general hospital, which encounter led her to go off and cut her throat with near success. She now wears a big bandage round it and is trying to bring herself to marry Dick Bartholomew, who offers security, love and a home in the country. Her heart is with Furneaux but she will soon marry Dick as she really has no other option.

Soon after this I do meet Vere again, washing his brushes in the room that is used for this purpose at the Chelsea School of Art. He greets me quite reasonably, asks me to come out and have some beer with him, and so our short but heavily dramatic relationship will now begin.

Vere comes trampling noisily down the stairs into John's room, insults John with laughing contempt and takes me off to spend the evenings drinking beer with him in various Chelsea pubs. I know that John has other girlfriends now, so there is no reason to feel guilty about my unfaithful behavior here.

Vere's amusement in the pubs is to pick out the most harmless looking citizen around and ply him with beer whilst relating the most fantastic 'there-I-was-upside-down' stories about himself during the war, which leaves the victim speechless and Vere and myself in hysterics.

Vere slops beer all over himself and everything nearby. He can't help this: all his movements are uncoordinated and he shakes terribly – but not from drink. He usually walks out quite suddenly, leaving the unwary citizen to pay the bill.

Vere drinks a lot of beer and relieves himself of it in the middle of the pavements any time he feels like it, quite regardless of passing citizens who have to jump into the road or doorways to avoid the deluge, which may or may not be actually aimed at them.

Presently he takes me on a bus to Kew where he has a big, bare, dirty attic in a very luxurious house. Here he relieves himself at length into the sink, shows me some of his canvasses and starts to draw me. He says – to my absolute astonishment – that I have the 'kindest' eyes he has ever seen and that he finds me very beautiful.

About the second or third time I come here (Vere is painting a picture of me now), he indicates the bed. I had expected this but I am dismayed by his expression. He looks wilder than ever, is not laughing and appears to be angry. He tries with angry, clumsy violence, to make love to me – fails repeatedly and finally chases me downstairs into the night, cursing horribly. I am quite unnerved by this and expect Vere is too since it is some days before he comes back for me again.

He has a splendid studio flat now, in a square off the Kings Road. Osbert and Edith Sitwell live opposite and I watch Edith, whose works I much admire, walking up and down the street looking like a long, black mushroom.

I spend much of my time here being painted by Vere during the day. He makes me sit quite still for hours and hours without a break, which is horribly exhausting but I do not dare move or he will hit me.

At night he continues trying to make love to me, cursing horribly and finally throwing me out of bed altogether. Mostly I have to sleep on the floor, since Vere will not let me back into the bed or out of the flat to sleep elsewhere.

This whole situation sounds ridiculous, but the fact is Vere and I are deeply and helplessly attached to each other. He is disgusted by the world in general and himself in particular, as, no doubt, am I. His behaviour towards me consists of terrifying mental brutality, suddenly followed by extraordinary tenderness, consideration and general expressions of love.

This treatment, when used as a device by psychiatrists, never fails to shatter me completely, even though I see it is coming and know exactly what is going on. I have unlimited admiration for Vere's paintings and in many ways for him, since I know by now a lot of the reasons for his behaviour and see the person underneath as truly loveable and fine and brave, imprisoned in dilemmas which he really cannot help.

Vere takes me to see 'Mummy', who lives in a luxurious flat in Sloane Square. Mummy is a small, rather unsympathetic-looking woman, while step-daddy is huge and charming. Both are clearly horrified to see us.

Vere tries to be reasonable but soon starts up shouting and cursing at Mummy, trampling around and around the room, breaking things up and making a mess. This always happens when we visit here together, but sometimes I go alone because I want to find out some things about Vere's life that he is not likely to tell the truth about.

Mummy tells me Vere went from his career in the Guards to be a Major in the Commandos during the war. Here he got a whole row of medals for unusually brave deeds, and blew up a German battleship singlehanded, which made him a real hero. Vere says this is nonsense – he always took a batman along to carry his hanky.

Mummy's main concern seems to be that Vere always used to change his shirt three times every day, used not to be in any way as he is now and she can't begin to think what is the matter with him. Well, I can. How would Mummy like to have spent all that time sticking knives into people, blowing them up and then have been expected to come home and carry on pruning roses for the flower show with her chum Lady Cadogan?

Vere has many other troubles too and our times together are getting more and more violently impossible. When he throws things at me or hits me and I ask him why, he says: 'Just for the hell of it!' - and hell indeed is just what this is.

Presently, after much drama and protest, I persuade Vere to consult Dr Westman about his problems with me in bed. Desperation drives him to it, and once there he is happy to go every day. Dr Westman tells me Vere has a very serious Oedipus complex that is going to take a long time for him to cure.

Having seen Vere in action with Mummy, I do not believe a word of this. Besides which, I know perfectly well what is the matter with Vere in this respect: it is simply that his sexual arrangements are about what you would expect from a fair-sized donkey and cannot be accommodated by anyone as undersized as me without a very off-putting struggle, which turns him off altogether.

This unfortunate accident of nature is a constant embarrassment to Vere, who says: 'It is no bloody use for anything at all except pissing out of!', which is doubtless why he does this so frequently in public. Well, if Vere is not going to explain this and Dr Westman has not the sense to find out, I shall have to try explaining it myself. So, when Dr Westman is well advanced with the Oedipus complex, I do tell him, in simple, basic terms, what the trouble really is.

Dr Westman sits quite speechless, while he tries to think of Vere and me as two human beings with a very basic problem, instead of as a collection of obscure complexes. Presently I see him actually smiling, and he comes out with: 'Vy not try some Vaseline then?'. Vy not, indeed. The outstanding simplicity of this solution to Vere's 20 years of misery leaves us both speechless. I can see at once that this is bound to work, and sure enough it does.

Vere is practically hysterical with delight, keeps on and on most of the time, and hardly ever lets me out of his sight. I am very happy for him, but my need to rest and recover is urgent now. I do not think I can go on like this for much longer – Vere is no different in any other respect – and I consider going back to Africa to rest with John.

Lying on John's bed one afternoon, trying to get some rest, I see him coming in looking strangely grim and determined. He sits down and tells me very firmly that he has had enough of me. He wants a reasonable, sane girl to live with, and gives me a week to clear off.

I hear what he is saying but cannot take it in for a long time. I had no idea he felt like this, and cannot believe he really means to leave me now, in this condition. But he goes on and on, telling me the same things over and over and then goes out to leave me here, crying myself into oblivion again. I am well and truly finished by this time, in every respect, and lie here thinking about nothing and feeling too ill to move.

Eventually I notice that my face feels very peculiar, my eyes hurt badly, and I am very hot and uncomfortable all over. I find that my face has gone blue - most of me has, in fact – and so, unsurprised by this, I lie down again and wait to die.

Some days later, the landlady sees me and calls the local doctor. He arrives, looks at me briefly and says I have a bad case of measles. He goes away again leaving neither treatment nor advice. He is fed up with non-paying, artistic vagrants, which is most of what his district consists of, and only sees us because he has to.

Michel appears briefly, looking horrified and offering some food, but I tell her to go away – she has enough trouble without my measles and I prefer to lie here and die as quickly as possible. One day the doctor comes back, says I am getting better and disappears for good.

Later, Vere arrives and is as nice as he can possibly be. He says I look like hell and he will take me for a holiday to any place in the world where I would like to go. I mention the Scilly Isles (I meant the Seychelles, but was too dazed to get the name right) and he says he will fix it for next week.

I try to wake up, clean myself up, eat something and get another little room nearby. Vere and I spend a week or two in the Scilly Isles, but the situation between us is so frightful that I manage to escape alone, back to the new little room in London, where I lie in a state of total despair and exhaustion, hoping never to see Vere again.

I think I should see Dr Westman now, but I know I cannot get there, so telephone Wolf who arrives with a bag of apples and a bottle of brandy, and takes me in a taxi to Marble Arch. Here Westman says I need a hospital at once, so Wolf gets me onto a train from which an ambulance collects me, somewhere in Cornwall.

The mental home is very nice indeed. It is an old manor house, where I have a beautiful room with flowers and pictures and everything is most comfortable and soothing. It is absolutely quiet and I never see any of the other patients except outside my window in this garden. For two or three days, I just lie here and cry without stopping at all and in such pain.

Then I see someone sitting quietly beside my bed – an elderly, serene Madonna, who now begins to talk to me. I don't know what this doctor's name is or remember what she says, but she could make anyone feel better by just sitting there and not saying anything at all. After some weeks, she takes me down to the beach and tells me to swim. It is so beautiful here, and I wish that I could stay, but presently this lovely lady tells me that I am better now: I understand things better and must try again.

Dr Westman, having inadvertently served some useful purpose to both Vere and I, is seen no more by any of us. To explain my evident hostility towards him, I recall the time when Michel went to see him in terrible distress, but having to say that she had no money to pay for his help. Considering the vast sums Papa was paying out for me, I thought he would ignore this for once at least. Michel says Westman then said he would take care of her mental problems in return for her taking care of his physical amusements, right there on his restful psychiatric couch.

Michel came back to me in tears – she was forced to make do with the collection of psychiatrists around the hospital, who then drove her to cut her throat.

We may have no morals, principles and such, but we do have strong feelings about what is fair and what is not. The idea of poor, fragile, desperate Michel in the clutches of that bloody-minded old goat made us all feel very hostile indeed.

In the train on the way back to London, I feel refreshed and optimistic. I think that I can manage now to leave Vere, go back to rest in Africa and leave the whole painful Chelsea scene forever. Michel has committed herself to Bartholemew, Wolf and John have developed other lives, and Vere...

Well, the first thing I see on arrival in my room is Vere, fast asleep on my bed. I do not remember what happens here, but the result is I say I will marry him, but it must be at once, and we must then go to Africa because otherwise I shall simply drop down dead.

Vere says he will arrange all this, and now treats me with much love and consideration. Having restored me somewhat with exotic food and drink, he now presents me with two hundred-pound notes and tells me to go to Harrods and get dressed, being sure to buy plenty of underclothes, which he assures me will have a suitable effect on him in the married state.

I take Michel with me to Harrods, so that she can get whatever she wants too, from this unexpected wealth. This expedition turns out very funny, since while I am trying out black underclothes in this reputable establishment, Vere and his equally disreputable friend Latham trample into my dressing room, both covered in paint and in very high spirits, to criticise or approve what is going on here. Between them, they decide on what I ought to have.

Vere is really being very thoughtful here, knowing that I am not be able to imagine what I ought to look like for getting married. He takes me back to a new and splendid apartment he has got for us in Chelsea.

On the morning of our wedding, Vere telephones Mummy, saying we are going to be married that day. We get ourselves to the Registry Office in The King's Road at more or less the right time, more or less suitably clothed, to find Mummy, Vere's brother Robert with his wife and child, Vere's brother Cecil, and reporters and photographers from just about every newspaper in London waiting for us.

Vere and I, supported by Latham and Michel, actually do get married that day, but the whole occasion is so nauseatingly public that Vere – fighting his way through reporters – takes off at once in a passing taxi for an unknown destination. It turns out later he went to recover in the National Gallery.

Latham has presented me with an ancient, dripping bunch of daffodils that have made a green river all down the front of my coat. Michel is silently distraught. Robert is noisily drunk. My only hope is Cecil, who appears to be reasonably composed.

Somehow Cecil gets the whole lot together at an Italian restaurant in Soho, which Vere has said is the only place where he might be willing to eat. Mummy has wanted to go to her home from home at The Ritz, but is shortly going to be very glad that we refused to go there.

Michael and Latham sensibly have left us by now, and step-daddy has even more sensibly declined to show up at all. Certain aspects of Vere's upbringing have stuck, compelling him to 'do the right thing' at certain unpredictable moments. So he turns up at the Italian restaurant at more or less the right time, though now wrapped up in his filthy old raincoat to hide the respectable suit he was obliged to wear for getting married. Also because Mummy has given him a truly splendid white raincoat for a wedding present.

Vere and I sit as far away from each other as possible. Mummy very solemnly presents me with a big box full of all the medals Vere has got for his Heroic Deeds. There is a deathly, solemn hush while I wait for Vere to blow up and the others wait for expressions of delight from me.

Beside me sits a handsome little boy done up in his Eton suit complete with topper (Robert's son) and I now present this disastrous box to him, feeling he might actually be pleased to have it and hoping thus to save the scene. Vere shrieks with laughter, the little boy loses his cool enough to be little-boyishly delighted, and the others are bereft of speech while they try to regain their composure.

This whole occasion goes on far too long – everyone is getting drunk and Vere ends up fighting with some stranger at another table who is complaining about the noise. The whole room is now in chaos. The little boy and I are staying put, trying to concentrate on admiring Vere's medals. The proprietor is flapping about like a wet hen and presently we find ourselves scattered about in the street.

Vere's upbringing has caused him to take a splendid room in a splendid hotel for our 'wedding night'. Here, knowing we are supposed to spend this night making love until we are overcome by sleep, we settle down lying head to feet on the bed.

Sometime during the night, Vere remembers that he is Catholic (converted) and says we must be married all over again in church or else we shall be 'living in sin'. He says I have to be a Catholic too for this and he takes me off to the Brompton Oratory to be instructed by a priest there who is well known to him. I go there six days running and find the priest and his dogmatic statements most indigestable.

I stick fast on having to promise to bring up my possible children as Catholics before they can be consulted about their own opinions, and the priest finally agrees to marry us in a side chapel of the Brompton Oratory. This apparently will make some difference and not upset his set of rules too much.

I do not remember too much about this wedding but the same people are there. I see Vere – on his knees, at some vital moment – turning out all his pockets onto the floor in the vain search for a 'piece of silver', which he is supposed to produce now and give to the priest, who is looking very sour indeed.

After this we all go to celebrate at Pruniers, which is actually much smarter than The Ritz, but Vere is now too exhausted to protest. Here he contents himself with rolling his eyes and saying, 'Wuff, wuff, wuff!' at anyone who speaks to him, which is his general habit when he is too tired to make a scene.

Both these weddings have been a heavy strain on me – in fact the whole thing is. I look forward only to getting onto the boat for Africa in one piece. But now, in our apartment, waiting for the boat, I feel a familiar sensation of burning all over and see that I am going blue again. This time it is chicken pox. It is the third time that childish ailments have turned up for me at particularly trying times. So of course we miss the boat.

Vere sits beside my bed drawing funny pictures for me and being as nice as he possibly can be. I hear him ordering the staff here and there to bring things up for 'my wife'. He has an absolutely deafening voice, with an Oxford accent so exaggerated that one might suppose he was putting it on if not familiar with his 'home' scene.

I know that he is trying out the term 'my wife' to see if he likes the idea of having a wife, and apparently finding he does. Seeing Vere as 'my husband' is an impossibility that I do not at any time attempt.

Chicken pox takes a few weeks to get over, but Vere has made arrangements for another boat. I send a cable to my Parents saying that I have got married and shall arrive with Vere on the Pretoria Castle. The ship sails off with us to worse and worse (though different) disasters in Africa, which I know are bound to happen but do not know at all how to prevent.

Chapter Eight

It is 1950 – I must be about 25 and Vere about 32.

On the *Pretoria Castle*, Vere is at once overcome by the idea that some other man on the ship might take an interest in me and so he locks me up in the cabin, bribes stewards not to come in and leaves me alone most of the time.

I lie on the top bunk trying to keep cool in every respect and look forward to mealtimes where Vere is obliged to let me out. Vere discovers that love-making on a narrow bunk with another one right on top of it is virtually impossible unless you have some idea how to do this in general, which he has not. So he spends his time with seamen in their part of the ship.

I see that he is getting very upset indeed, and fear that he or I, or both, will go right out of our minds before we ever get to Africa. I also see that if we do get there, Vere is going to find himself in a situation that he will possibly not be able to bear, even if he should decide to try, which is unlikely.

He does not let me out at Tenerife, which is an island I enjoy, or at Cape Town, which comes next. The ship has just left Cape Town when there is a sudden, very violent storm. The waves get more and more gigantic and there is deafening noise as everything on the ship falls about, and the grand piano upstairs goes clean through the roof of the saloon. Passengers are screaming with terror, and the stewards say this ship is so top-heavy that it will certainly capsize.

I see Vere standing in the doorway looking very frightened indeed, and realize he is not putting this on because he is actually wetting his pants in rivers all over the floor, shaking most terribly and quite unable to speak.

But I am not afraid of this kind of danger, I am much enjoying it in fact. I drag Vere upstairs onto the deck – no easy matter since the ship is practically standing on its head. Here, lying flat and holding onto something solid, we can enjoy this spectacle and also hope to be thrown off the ship when it turns over instead of going down with it.

Well, it does not turn over after all, and now Vere spends his time in the cabin with me, trying to recover but not being able to until we get to Durban.

Here I see Parents, Julian and my sister standing on the quay, waiting for us. But Vere locks himself up in the cabin and flatly refuses to come out, which leads to a confusing encounter with my relatives who want to know who, what, why and particularly where about my husband, straight away. Eventually some member of the crew forces Vere to come out, and his first encounter with my family is so disastrous I hardly remember anything about it.

Parents now live in a house in Ridge Road and have prepared a room with its own bathroom and verandah here for Vere and I to stay in. He starts at once to paint pictures of me all day long, so that I still stay shut up except for mealtimes.

Vere mostly refuses to come to meals at all, and is just as rude to my parents as he can possibly be. He is truly terrible to me and I am now truly terrified of him. Parents are unnerved, and Julian, now 13, sees Vere kick me very hard one day and hurls himself at Vere, kicking and fighting as hard as he can. Vere does not retaliate to this but just stands still, looking awful.

Vere puts on my bathing costume, which is black-and-white one-piece with built-in bra, and disappears in this and nothing else for three days. Returning early one morning, still in the bathing costume and looking very wild, he says he has been staying with Mama's friend Mrs Lasson, 'having sex with her mostly on the beach'. Knowing Mrs Lasson, this is likely to be true.

Vere now becomes somewhat obscene. He lies on the bed stark naked in the evenings, with all the lights on, making rude gestures with his body at passers-by in the street outside our open window, calling out to make sure they see what he is up to. He ought to be laughing about this, characteristically, but he is not. He is looking grim and terrible, and female shrieks now heard in the street make me afraid he is going to get into trouble.

He has stopped painting and spends much of the time sitting in the lavatory with his pants down, cursing and making faces at everyone in the house (except Julian), who can't help seeing him from the corridor because all the doors must be kept open.

Vere is frightening himself by now. He says that since he is in this unspeakable country, he had better draw some wild beasts. He gets a station wagon, which he cannot or will not drive. We set off for Hluh-luwe game reserve, calming down a bit on the way.

Here, on the very first day, Vere tells me to stop the car halfway up a very steep, rocky, little track because he has seen a very big black rhino standing in the long grass nearby. He leans over and keeps on blowing the horn at this creature until it suddenly charges out of the grass and up the hill at us. Our guide in the back of the car is shrieking with terror, while Vere is shrieking with laughter.

I have much trouble getting started and away fast enough to save us from the most horrible sort of death I could imagine. I am abso-lutely terrified of wild beasts under any circumstances and am now so shaken up that Vere takes pity on me and we go back to Durban.

Here there is such a terrible scene one afternoon that I run out of the house and disappear into the dark space underneath it, where I lie writhing about in the dust, crying out and presumably having some sort of fit. I see Mrs Lasson crouched there in the space I came in through, and hear her screaming at what she sees and hears of me.

She has hysterics and bolts. Later, I see and hear my old friend Sandy Cuthbert there and he tells me quietly to come out, carries me back to the house and puts me to bed. Presently I find that Sandy's wife Christine is sitting beside me on the bed. She tells me that Sandy is talking to Vere (I can hear Vere shouting in the distance) and will come back soon and put me to sleep again.

It is late at night now, and when Sandy does come back I tell him that I do have a most awful pain, and believe that I have been preg-nant for some while. I should have been prepared for this, having never in my life made any sort of attempt to avoid it other than hope-ful monthly prayers – but I was not.

Sandy finds out this is true and takes me off at once to Parklands Nursing Home. Here I lie for some days with horrible tubes hanging out of various bits of my body. Sandy is often here, and once I see him talking to another doctor called McMahon about me. Presently Sandy tells me I have TB once again and he is going to remove my baby be-cause I am in no fit state to continue having it.

Now Vere is sitting beside my bed, trying hard to look composed, and cheer me up. He says he is laughing because he is enjoying being 'a father', for this day at least, but I see the tears in his eyes and have a most truly painful idea of what he is really feeling. He has brought me a most beautiful picture that he has been painting of me and I think our mutual pain at this point is truly total.

Now Sandy has removed the baby and I lie on a bed in the garden at Parents' house. Sandy has told Vere that if he does not go away at once I shall most certainly die for one reason or another right now, so Vere does go away, to Paris.

I do not want to stay here having TB all over again – I want to go to Paris with Vere and hope he will be better there. But since I can hardly even move I have to be content with saying I will get better as quickly as possible and join him in Paris. I do not remember saying goodbye to Vere and think it likely that we preferred to avoid this altogether. He must have gone while I was still at Parklands.

So now I lie in the garden or in another little room in this house. Sandy or Dr Harry Curwen come three times every day to give me injections of Streptomycene for the next three months.

Often Sandy will stay to play a game of chess with me, while Harry often stays to keep me company after the evening injection. He has other games in mind for me but, though we both are well aware of this, I am not going to find myself in bed with him for some time yet.

Harry likes to drink, but he will not do so until after six o' clock in the evening, when we both drink quite a lot together, enjoying each other's company as much as our equally disastrous lives allow. Parents, seeing that Harry is cheering me up, always leave us alone, whether we are at the house or driving in Harry's car.

Mama is having a disastrous affair with a well-known photographer in Durban, which leads to hideous and public consequence, where Papa is called upon to get her out of it. Papa is trying to be a photographer in Durban himself, hoping no doubt to keep out of the house as much as possible.

Three months go by and I am now supposed to be better, after all that Streptomycene. But I am not better at all and Sandy says I must go to a sanitorium somewhere to be cured of the TB at least. My feeling about this is that if I am shut up once again in a sanitorium I shall never get out of it again. Besides, I never really believed in the TB diagnosis anyway, I flatly refuse to go to any sort of sanitorium, and so Papa buys a big farm in Greytown where the air will be better for me and the outdoor life should do me good.

So, with my marriage to Vere now more or less over and the first of my four babies duly dead, I set off with Parents and Julian for the healthy life on a farm, of all things, in Greytown.

Chapter Nine

The farm turns out to be a large, with a dilapidated old house.

Papa is enchanted by the plant that grows right through the wall into his room. The farm has a beautiful dam and various outbuildings, one of which has been made habitable for me, since I flatly refuse to live in the same house with Parents ever again. Besides the many acres of vegetation, there are many assorted kinds of cows, ducks, and hundreds of very confused hens, which have escaped and taken refuge in the trees.

Papa, seeing there is nothing he can possibly do about any of this, gets himself a studio in Greytown and carries on trying to be a photographer there. Mama, who has always said she is a country girl at heart, gets a big black horse on which she gallops about the farm, urging unwilling labourers to do whatever it is presumed they may know what needs to be done. Julian and I, trying to be helpful, shoot at the hens in the trees with his air-gun, trying to catch and shut them up again. This situation has no bearing on my narrative other than to show the general confusion and explain why Papa ended up more or less destitute.

I like my outbuilding and try to settle down there to paint, recover my health and enjoy Julian's company. He goes daily to a convent in Greytown, to be helped by some kindly nun to pass exams that an erractic education and his life in general have made impossible for him to do in the usual way.

Presently a young man turns up, asking permission to shoot ducks on our dam with Julian and me. He is a pleasant, amusing sort and now spends most of his days and nights with me. This seems natural and uncomplicated to me, since I have no feelings other than a vague sort of general liking for his company.

But he stands beside my bed one night, saying that I am the first and only true love of his life, and what am I going to do about this? What I do is tell him to go away at once, and stay away, since having anything at all to do with me is only going to cause him pain.

About this time, Mama's friend Bill comes to stay quite often. He spends the nights running backwards and forwards between Mama's bedroom and mine, evidently much amused by this. He is conventionally handsome, utterly revolting, and currently, I think, in prison.

It seems he was not quite revolting enough, because I now spend time visiting two old men in the village. One of these appears to think he is well disposed to me, the other is simply a dirty old man and does not pretend to be much else.

Of these two, the first is actually the most revolting, an ancient giant with yellow teeth and big black glasses. So I spend most of the time with him, lying naked on his bed. Neither of them could achieve their main objective with me, since I was absolutely petrified with horror about these situations, which I knew to be of my own making but for what reason I had no idea. I was not even drunk, or would not remember all of this with such painful clarity as I do now.

I am still physically ill and a young man comes to give me sedatives and general treatment. He provides Seconals and Luminals but his main object is always 'having sex' with me, here in my room. I say nothing about this until, overcome by curiosity. I ask him exactly what he is doing this for? He says because it is good for me, carries on as usual, and I conclude Mama is keeping watch.

One night I notice that I have a good supply of Seconals and Luminals and feel the best thing I can do is swallow the whole lot and go to sleep for good. I remember walking around my room that night, wondering if this is the best way to do it and contemplating the very primitive furnace outside my window.

I suppose this looked too painful and so I swallowed all the pills I had and then composed myself in bed for what I hoped was final sleep. I probably expected to wake up again in heaven, having not yet lost sight of such beliefs, thinking always much about them and feeling that, where the predicaments of my life might be truly understood, I could still hope to be forgiven and so live happily ever after somewhere else. Or at least have a chance to start again differently.

The next thing I know it is daytime and the young man is trying to make me walk round and round my room, giving me injections from time to time, and talking to Mama, who is standing about, making a noise.

There is a total blank now, ending up with my asking Sandy to please cut me open and see what might be causing me the most terrible pains that I have now. Sandy comes at once to do this operation on me. Knowing the effect hospital surroundings are likely to have on me, Sandy puts me in a private room with a private nurse.

This is an old woman, not in uniform, since Sandy also knows that if a young woman of any sort should even put her hand on me I should become positively violent. This remark might seem pointless, but will be shown later to have considerable importance for me and others. The result of these arrangements is that the general staff of this hospital have nothing to do with me at all at this time.

The day before this operation, I am drinking alone on the verandah of the local hotel when I get into conversation with a young man I hardly know, who now shows much interest in me and what is about to happen tomorrow. I see that Roger is a remarkably good looking, lively and generally attractive boy, but I am in no mood to be amused and think nothing much about this encounter.

Sandy puts me to bed in hospital and then to sleep with assurances that I shall not know anything much more until I am at home again. Waking up after this operation, I see Sandy standing beside me laughing and looking very pleased.

He says I have a visitor, and lets in Roger, who is in very high spirits and wearing a funny leather helmet because he has been playing football. Sandy and the nurse go out now, and Roger at once lies down on my bed and holds me in his arms, providing much needed comfort whilst he laughs and sings and tells me of his game of football, polo or whatever it was this day.

Roger is warm and very loving. For the three weeks I stay here, he comes every day and stays most of the night as well, always lying on my bed with me in his arms. I enjoy his funny talk and am fully aware of all the peace and rest and positive happiness (when was I last really happy?) that this so unexpectedly brings for me.

Sandy is very pleased. He says there was nothing seriously wrong with my insides, which he has taken out and spread about on the operating table to make sure. He now prepares me to go home again.

Roger and I do not wish to be parted from each other, so when Mama comes to fetch me home she finds him waiting with his suitcase, ready to come home with me. She unaccountably is annoyed about this but bears it all the same and puts Roger and his belongings in another outbuilding near to mine.

So now I lie in my own bed with my middle (cut from my navel down as far as possible) held together with bandages and not causing me much pain, since Roger is a constant pleasure and amusement, trying here to paint.

Since he spends nights with me, I suppose it is inevitable that he should end up restive and wanting to make love to me. This event cannot be satisfactory, since we are both alarmed by the likely prospect of my middle bursting open again at the wrong moment, so we only tried once.

After Roger has been here about a week, his father – looking very angry and making a terrible scene – comes to fetch him and send him off to London at once, to be a TV actor, which is what he wants most of all, as his father very well knows. Well, it was nice while it lasted, but we both knew this could not be long. I am very sad to lose this charming boy, but also much relieved to find myself now free of horrible compulsions and able to continue to paint in peace.

Peace lasts for about one more week and then I wake up at 4.30 one morning with the same sort of pain I had on the Dutch boat, but now a great deal worse. I am screaming with pain, vomiting all the time and falling about on the floor. My new doctor takes me at once back to hospital, where I continue screaming and vomiting with pain for the next 24 hours (except for brief respites, from morphia injections that soon wear off). At exactly 4.30 the pain suddenly disappears.

Knowing it will not come back again, I get out of bed and telephone Parents to come and fetch me home. Some nurse saw me doing this, got me back to bed and called Dr Haupt at once. So he sits by my bed in the dark and talks for a long time.

He says there are no physical reasons for what has happened but that if it happens again at the wrong time I should most likely die. I don't suppose I believe him, but I go on to take the extra sedatives he gives me and stay quietly alone, painting in my room.

I am trying to make it clear in my letters to Vere that I cannot face the prospect of life with him again and do not intend to try. He will not accept this and sends his brother Cecil down from Nigeria to talk me into going back to him.

Cecil is supposed to stay here for three weeks, and for the first three does do his best to talk me into going back to Vere. This would have been more painful than it was, had Cecil been less generally and obviously idiotic. Julian and I, noting the hairclips that keep Cecil's curls in place, and finding him altogether intolerable, tip him off our raft into the dam, judging accurately that this will get rid of him at once.

Vere now becomes even more pressing. But I – trying to make my feelings absolutely clear – ask for a divorce. This argument goes on and on for a long time, ending with my agreeing to go back to London and talk to Vere about it.

I do not want to go and say I only will if he sends me a return ticket and agrees to see me in London only in public places, where he will not be able to either throw me into bed or make too many awful scenes. My ticket arrives at once, with expressions of much delight from Vere, and so once again…

It is March 1951 and it is the Athlone Castle this time. I am in a very unbalanced condition altogether but propose to enjoy this voyage one way or another and avoid thinking about what is going to happen when I see Vere again.

When the ship sails out of Durban, I fall to pieces almost at once, take far too many Seconals as soon as I wake up, and hope to sleep for a day or two and wake up feeling better. But I am woken up after only a few hours by a stewardess, followed by the arrival of the ship's doctor, who is very bad tempered, taking a very dim view indeed of what he thinks to be an attempt at suicide. I go upstairs to sleep it off in the saloon where I am very soon picked up by a man who appears perfectly reasonable but in fact is not.

I spend the rest of this voyage mostly lying on my bed, hot and dazed, and probably drunk and naked, with this man whose name I cannot even remember. One of his many peculiarities is that every time he has finishes having sex with me (which is all day, every day) he falls down flat on his face and bursts into floods of tears, which he seems quite unable to control. I never find out why he does this, but remember being interested enough to wonder.

The evenings we spend with the other passengers, all being very gay and apparently reasonable. At night, he sleeps in his own cabin with his daughter, who is ten years old, motherless and apparently afraid of the dark.

Arriving at Southampton, I look out of my window to see if Vere is there among the waiting crowds. He is not, but I see him coming up the crew's gangway with a collection of stevedores, which he can easily get away with since he is looking more filthy and delapidated than ever. I leave my cabin in much haste and meet Vere trampling about in the saloon. He is in a very excitable state, much delighted to see me again and being as nice as he possibly can be.

I simply cannot remember anything about getting to London nor what happens when we do. I can't even remember where I spend the night but I do not think it was with Vere. I remember getting a room in Beaufort Street, Chelsea, which I hardly ever occupy. Also that Vere and I arrange to meet most days in a squalid little coffee bar in the Kings Road.

This place is always filled with artistic vagrants, who sit here doing crossword puzzles and waiting for someone to produce a cigarette, coffee or food to keep them going. So I sit here doing puzzles too, fortunately provided with plenty of money from Vere, but not able to think of anywhere else to go or anything else to do.

After some time like this, a really bad-looking character comes into focus, talking to me. He has long, thick, yellow hair and a beard, a heavy build, and big, blue, frozen, empty eyes staring out of a Slavonic type of face. We have a short conversation about nothing in particular. I note his interest in my South African cigarettes and probable belief that I am a rich South African tourist and an obviously easy lay. He then gets up and says – well, shall we walk or take a taxi? We take a taxi to his room, and so my fortunately fairly brief encounter with Zola begins.

He has a remarkably pleasant room (by which I mean that it feels nice, besides being quite comfortable and clean), where I now spend much of my time. Zola is engaged in faking antiques, when he is not occupied in bed with various old ladies who pay him for this, or other such dealings which save him from actually having to work.

I help him with faking antiques (interesting), cook our meals here mostly, provide him with money whenever he asks for it, and usually sleep here either with or without him. Zola is either too lazy or simply too uninterested to bother much about sex with me, so this aspect of our curious relationship is really not relevant to me.

Sometimes his wife telephones from Scotland to ask me if he is all right and if he is as bloody as usual. He has burnt himself rather badly by falling asleep under a sun lamp, so I can only tell his wife that he is even more bloody than usual. I don't think I need say much more about H, except that I became curiously fond of him. He ended up by saying with evident sincerity that I was the only good thing that ever happened in his life.

Of course I do see my old friends too. John Kevan comes to my room looking very haggard and destitute. I ask if he has changed his mind and would like to come back to Africa with me. He has not and will not, although I think I wish he would.

I go to visit Michel at her house in the country, but find myself unable to communicate with her at all and go away at once. Hazel comes to London to see me and lends me, for comfort, I suppose, a very valuable sovereign case with sovereigns and gold chain, which Zola promptly pawns and does not get back for me.

I feel so bad about this that I am not able even to write to Hazel again. She is so innocent and could not possibly be expected to understand any part of this, since she truly believes that people in general – and me in particular – are fundamentally good.

I go to Seaford to visit my Aunt Doris, of whom I have always been most fond. She has taken to being a British Israelite and so we explore endless maps of the Great Pyramid together, while she tells me all about the awful fate that is in store for the awful sinners any moment now.

I visit Conrad in his studio, which has more or less collapsed for good. He is patching a hole in the roof with a painting that his neighbour Mathew Smith has given him for this purpose, and which he could have sold for more than enough money to buy the entire place.

The wife and child have disappeared and Conrad looks badly in need of repairs, so I tell him to go visit my Aunt Doris, who may rest and feed him up. He goes there at once and frequently thereafter since they take to each other very much.

Of course, in all these years I have never really managed to forget a single thing about my life with Wolf. He lives right here in Beaufort Street, only a few houses away from mine, as I knew very well when I came here.

I pass his house every day and sometimes I go up to his room, where we talk and drink coffee. I never stay for long. We have been writing to each other all the time and I know that Wolf believes I shall go back to him when I have finished 'fooling about' somewhere else. I am very inclined to believe this myself, and very much aware of him watching and waiting to see what will happen when I get divorced from Vere.

I think I stay in England for about nine months this time. Towards the end, Vere finally is convinced that nothing will make me stay with him and perhaps he now realizes our original feelings for each other are now extinct. So he agrees to the divorce.

We go together to Lincolns Inn to consult Dr Jacobi, who is amused by us. He says the only quick and sensible way for us to divorce is for Vere to commit adultery. Vere is stunned with terror by this suggestion – says he has no idea how to pick up a tart or what to do with her if he did.

In the end, Jacobi has to arrange the whole thing himself, sending a suitable girl round to Vere's studio at breakfast time and a well-primed detective who will be sure to give them enough time to arrange themselves in bed after he has knocked on the door. All three end up having breakfast together. Vere's account of this to me is very funny indeed.

I can go back to Africa again and Vere, having given me a thousand pounds and a reasonably cheerful farewell embrace, goes back to France.

I have told Wolf that I am going and now return to his room to say goodbye. He is sitting cross-legged on his bed in his underpants, with a black silk stocking over his head, rocking to and fro and looking mad all over again.

As I stand here, a wild-looking, red-haired woman called Sarah comes in. She seems to know what to do about Wolf, and tells me an ambulance is on the way to take him to some mental hospital outside of London.

My ship is leaving the next day, but I take a train to the mental hospital to see Wolf lying there looking exactly as he did with the stocking over his head. I kiss him goodbye and run away as fast as I can. It may be Wolf is trying to stop me going again, but it is very real and very terrible indeed.

I remember Zola getting up energy to take me to Southampton and leaving me there with some regret. But the voyage back I can hardly remember at all. I am very tired and very sick, and stay alone in my cabin mostly all the way to Durban, arriving there some time in 1952.

Chapter Ten

Waking up early one morning in my room at the farm at Greytown, I see the sun shining on the hills outside, my brother walking about there looking familiar and dependable, and feel astonished to find myself positively happy to be here and alive.

I lie here thinking about this for quite some time and then get up and start to paint. From this moment until I come to Fort Napier mental hospital in 1957, I paint every day from early morning until whatever time I fall asleep exhausted in the afternoon. Evenings and much of the nights, I spend awake, either alone or with other people.

My companions here in Greytown are two painters – Alex Wagner and Cassim Lakki – and their wives, as well as an ex-pilot who turns up from time to time. He has had a freak accident by falling out of his airplane during the war and landing quite unhurt in a hay cart. His hair turned snow white on the way down and he says he had plenty of time to think about life in general then.

I do not particularly like the Wagners or the Lakkis. Cassim has an astounding collection of books and works of art, while Alex is making a good living painting special pictures for wealthy people. They all seem to think our evenings at Cassim's house are very wild, but if they are, I have no part in this at all.

The pilot, whom I do like, stays safely on the other side of my room, and shows much interest in my paintings. It is he who first suggests that I should have an exhibition of my paintings in Durban. This thought has never occurred to me but now I feel inclined to try. Some exhibitions entail endless difficulties that can only be overcome properly by experience, but my sister, who lives in Durban, helps me here.

So, in May 1953, I go off to Durban with some of my paintings in my car, to have my first exhibition there. I stay alone at the Royal Hotel, sell one or two pictures, am astonished and much gratified by my critics and am determined to be a painter, no matter what.

This is a very big moment in my life. Relief, perhaps, from an endless chain of humiliations of one sort or another, and what I remember of my feelings then is the strongest word that can be used for 'surprise'.

During my few days here, I take time off to visit an exhibition Sister Plentia is holding in a gallery nearby. I notice a very familiar little man who is smiling and clearly wanting to talk to me. I say familiar because he looks like all the refugees I ever knew and liked so much, made up into one person.

He has a big head on a wasted, battered, body – a very comic, battered sort of face, and the most beautiful eyes, which are here looking at me with much enthusiasm. We talk a bit and I tell him where I am staying and the number of my room. That evening, Bernard comes there and gets straight into bed with me. I expected this and thought of it as a necessary introduction to someone I was clearly going to like.

But later, to my absolute consternation, he tells me he has fallen in love with me on sight, will never love anyone else in his life, and what am I going to do about this? Well, I just did not believe him. He is much older than me, has a wife who sounds formidable, a little boy whom he clearly loves, and he looks quite able to take care of himself. In any case, all my thoughts are concentrated on my exhibition and my future life as primarily a painter. I don't remember what is said but do know I do not expect to see him again.

Back in Greytown, I continue painting with more concentration than ever, whilst whole masses of red roses arrive for me at intervals during the weeks, and then Bernard himself arrives to stay with me most weekends.

My mistake here is that I never do take Bernard seriously. I am pleased enough to see him when he turns up, really enjoy his company, am totally indifferent to his lovemaking and really do not think much about any of this at all.

My life goes on like this for about a year, during which the only 'incident' I remember is the arrival of two private detectives in the middle of one night asking for Bernard. Thinking they are stranded motorists, I show them Bernard lying in my bed asleep.

He seems more annoyed than surprised and is not much upset by the subsequent divorce, since he did not much like his wife anyway and can still see his little boy. But now he wants to marry me, in spite of my telling him repeatedly that I do not love him, never will, and shall most likely go back to Wolf one day. Bernard often bursts into tears and I wish – with some regret – that he would go away. In fact it is I who go away now, since my Parents wish to leave this farm and go to live in Pinetown. I do not know what it is that goes wrong with me at this point, but something does go very wrong indeed.

In Pinetown, Mama and Julian live in the house, Papa is in Amsterdam (I have no idea why), and I live in the garage which has been converted into a studio flat for me. My garage is very big, very dark (I can't remember anything except the dimmest sort of light in there) and the walls are covered with my pictures, which I am painting as usual all the time.

Bernard still turns up quite often, looking miserable and about to give up. Julian and I keep each other company until one evening when we tell our Mama we are going to the cinema together. She bursts into tears, makes a terrible scene, and says we are selfish and terrible to spend our time together instead of with her. We are fed up, but know that nothing on earth will stop her doing this, and so do not go out together and see much less of each other.

Julian goes off to work in a night club and presently brings a friend to visit me. This young man is very good looking, very 'neurotic' indeed, and to me, nearly always very unpleasant. He comes to see me most evenings and I am always pleased to see him. Once or twice we spend some time in bed together, but I remember this being actually too unpleasant for me.

Now quite suddenly Mama is very ill indeed. She lies in bed crying out with pain (absolutely uncharacteristic) and telling me she is going to die, and what I am to do when she is dead, and how much she always loved me, and so on and so on. I am alone in the house with her and cannot get Sandy because it is Sunday and he is somewhere playing golf.

By the time he actually does turn up Mama's appendix has burst, she looks nearly dead and I am shocked absolutely witless. So now Mama is recovering at the Marianhill Mission but, after a day or two, I find myself quite unable to recover at all. I cannot stop crying, see the mental hospital coming up all over again and phone Sandy to come and help me.

Sandy is looking angry, sounding angry, and actually shaking me. He talks a long time, and part of what he says is that Julian and I see far too much of each other – we are 'all charm and worth nothing at all' and our relationship is 'unhealthy'. At this, I make the fatal mistake of taking offence and refusing to see Sandy ever again – until years later when I know I am going to have Antonia and realize that taking offence about anything at all is a mistake.

I do not know why Sandy was so unkind and silly that day, but presume the shock and anger he aroused did at least stop me crying. Such emotions as I might have left are now completely frozen and will stay that way for quite some time.

My unpleasant young man now arrives one evening with a friend of his called Timothy, whom he has told is more than welcome to see me since he has another girl in mind. I look at Timothy with much dislike and tell him to stand on his head. Which he does. I tell him to fix my fire. Which he does. I tell him to keep on turning records on my gramophone, go and cut off his moustache, go and make me coffee… all of which he does with a cheerful smile. I tell him to go away and get lost, which he never has done.

Timothy comes to see me every evening now, on his motorbike. He looks around for whatever he can do to be helpful to me: fixes the gramophone so it will keep playing the same record (French cabaret music) over and over all the time, which is what I want it to do; and mends broken things that are lying about.

He talks away cheerfully about what he has been doing, reading, seeing or anything like that. I do not answer him, or talk to him, and think I wish he would go away. It is some weeks or months, maybe, before I notice one evening that I am listening for the motorbike to come and caring a bit whether it does or not. I lock my door at once, and Timothy, finding it so, goes home straight away.

The next day he comes back just as usual, and he sits quite near me by the fire and we talk to each other more about things that are important to us both. I discover his father died when he was very small, leaving him with an alcoholic mother who has given him a very awful life indeed.

Timothy is also sick from a motor accident he had at Michael-house, the private school, which has left him with a good deal of his backbones all stuck together, as well other, permanent wounds. None of which he ever speaks about, even when quite green with pain.

I have noticed a little boy, about 12, I suppose, who stands in the road every day staring at me painting in the window of my garage. One day I call to him to come in if he wants to see what I am doing. I tell him to sit down somewhere behind me and talk if he wants to.

So Derek sits here with me talking about the problems of his life, while he watches how to become a painter, which is what he wants to be. Soon Derek is painting his own pictures here with me, understanding everything I tell him, and doing it so very well that we are both immensely proud of him.

His father is not pleased but does not forbid him from coming here, and so he spends as much time as he can with me all the time that I am still in Pinetown. Derek turns up later in my life, festooned with jewellery, clearly gay and running a disco where he plays piano. He ends up causing his father more trouble than he would have done if left to pursue his natural inclinations in peace!

Timothy brings his friend Neil Sack to see me sometimes and we are considering another exhibition for me. In May 1955 I think it is now time for this, since my walls are overflowing with pictures and I am aware that something is 'wrong' with me which might possibly be improved in this way.

Papa (I do not remember his reappearance at all) brings his friend, the author Alan Paton, to see what he thinks of my paintings and if he will open my exhibition for me at the International Club in Durban. I don't know what Mr Paton actually thinks of my paintings, but he becomes a good friend to me.

I now have my exhibition, which I try very hard to enjoy but in fact do not. I sell quite a few pictures and the critics are enthusiastic as usual, but I think the whole thing in general – and me trying to present the required image as 'the artist' is so phony that I end up feeling worse than ever.

I do not remember how long after that we stayed in Pinetown or what may have happened there. The next thing I do remember is trying to fix up another outbuilding for myself in the garden of a house at Penzance Road in Durban, which is where my Parents have moved to now.

My father is working at the African YMCA in Beatrice Street. Mama is mostly in the house. Julian is heard by me weeping most bitterly one night in his room in my cottage, where he stays when out of work. Timothy has a new and splendid motorbike (he is passionately addicted to these) and is trying to paint.

He spends every moment that he possibly can with me, offering always everything I most need and want, but never will accept. I try to settle down to paint here 'as usual', but I am now on an absolutely straight, unbroken line toward Fort Napier mental hospital, which I know is coming soon in one shape or another, but do not know or care how to keep away.

In Penzance Road, I paint longer hours every day, with the same record playing over and over all the time, and other people often sitting around talking while I paint. I want it this way so that my mind will be distracted from what I am doing with my hand, which is clearly more reliable.

I join the Natal Society of Artists, being made a member at once, which is considered an honour. It means I can – and do – hang five pictures in any of their exhibitions instead of the usual two.

I drink gallons of thick black coffee all day long and probably a good deal of brandy as well, certainly at night. I have a little car now, because I am afraid to drive the big one so fast as I always do.

Timothy says he has met a girl he likes very much indeed. She is a brilliant commercial artist, very amusing and she is a lesbian. Timothy looks a bit dubious about this bit, but I am curious to know what sort of person this might be, and tell him to bring her around.

Wendy looks like a mischievous little girl to me. She has a mop of black curls, violently striped silk pants, and starts up dancing the Charlston to amuse me in my room. I am very amused indeed and much attracted to this girl at once.

Wendy asks us to a party in her flat on the beachfront. Here I see many boys dressed up as girls, girls dressed up as boys, and Wendy making her intentions towards me perfectly obvious. Having always understood that to be 'queer' is not only unfortunate but positively wrong, I am most surprised to see that all these people appear to be enjoying themselves very much, and are very nice and very friendly towards me. Timothy is looking fed up, somewhat sick, and goes home.

Thinking about this after the party, I can see no proper reason why it should matter what sex a person should happen to be, in any sort of relationship, and so decide to pursue my friendship with Wendy in whatever way she wants.

Wendy is warm and gay, and very, very loving indeed. She is also violently temperamental and much given to emotional storms of tears and rages when – after some months – I find that in spite of not seeing any reason for it, I simply cannot be a lesbian myself.

I cannot stand the endless scenes. I find the people I thought to be so happy together are actually jealous, possessive, hysterical and generally bloody-minded to each other most of the time. I am really very fond of Wendy all the same, and her true devotion to me leads us to a situation where she, Timothy and I all have a very close and reasonable relationship with each other.

However, this is a very bad time for all of us while it lasts. I still continue going to the 'queer' parties, and they still accept me and are very kind and friendly. I do go to many ordinary parties as well, usually alone.

A young American called Bill is having parties all the time in his flat. He looks like everybody's idea of a Hollywood film star, and says he is a photographer and also writing a film script here. Many of the people at his endless parties are of different races (such mixing is very rare in South Africa at this time) and include Liberal Party members, African National Congress members and so on, most of whom I know.

I have a feeling there is something odd about Bill and am sceptical about his stories, but he takes a beautiful photograph for me of my friend Selby, a black painter, so I know he is a photographer at least.

Presently Bill asks me to come out with him alone. He is looking very smooth and elegant, and after a very dimly-lit, elegant dinner, we sit on his elegant, black suede sofa in suitably dim light, listening to suitably dim music, for a little while. Of course, I know what is to happen, but when it does am absolutely horrified to find Bill, of all people, collapsed all over me in floods of tears, hanging on to me in desperation, saying over and over, 'Please don't go away, don't leave me', and so on and on. This whole episode is so bizarre that I simply bolt at once and never go back.

Leaving aside this unfortunate young man, there are two who come to spend nights with me quite often. These are large, and warm, and comfortable, and both much addicted to playing football and such things.

My closest friends, aside from Timothy and Wendy, are Selby and Zainab, an Indian painter. There are also the artist Stuart Campbell, some of Timothy's friends, a girl I used as a model and various others. None of whom gets into bed with me except for Timothy, who sometimes does, but since this always makes me cry it does not happen often.

Wandering around the fairground on the beach one night, I come across a very young Hungarian artist. Rolf is a wood carver, but otherwise dirty, stupid and generally awful.

So I take him home with me for a few months, on and off, until I find that I am going to have his baby. So now what? I ask my Parents to my room together, explain this situation and ask what they would like me to do about it. They don't know. I don't know. There is general confusion.

Now Timothy, who can't even stand the sight of Rolf, comes to my room dressed in a suit, bringing flowers for me in his hand. He kneels on the floor in front of me and asks me from the very bottom of his heart please to do him the honour to become his wife.

I know so well that indeed he will look after me – and Rolf's child – with absolute devotion for all the rest of my life. I know that I can never love him as he wants me to and I know just what life with me may do to him. I know very well what I am doing when I say to Timothy, all right then, thank you very much, I will.

I do not know why it was that we did not get married straight away, but I was five months' pregnant when my sickness, pains and fever became so acute that I felt sure my baby was about to come unstuck. In Addington hospital, no one believed a single word I said and put me to bed there for 'observation' with no treatment whatsoever – until the morning, when I showed them my dead baby (another boy, it was), lying in my bed.

So now they do believe me. I lie here for another two weeks seeing all kinds of doctors and, I think, a psychiatrist. Timothy comes to see me whenever he can, and takes me home again with a big bottle of Phenol Barbitol and bella donna, which I am to take all the time and get refilled at Addington each week. This mixture actually works, my pains disappear, I feel much relieved, and presently make it clear to Timothy that I am not going to marry him at after all.

There is relative peace for a little while, and I continue to paint and live as usual until the pains start coming back again. I take more and more medicine, and very soon cannot walk straight, see straight or keep awake.

In my car with Wendy, I run straight into the side of a stationary car parked in a practically deserted Umbilo Road. I do not stop, but go as fast as I can to fall flat on my bed at home. Wendy says I must tell Papa about this, and so I do, and hear no more about it except that he fixed this matter up.

But now I do not take any medicine at all and so feel very sick indeed. Parents now produce a whole variety of quacks to see if they can make me well.

Dr Vandeburg (as I shall call him) is a faith healer, but since I have lost sight of faith in anything at all he soon gives up. Mr Jones (as I shall call him) is also a faith healer and also soon gives up. Mr Smith (as I shall call him) is a palmist who absolutely turns me up. A well-known fortune teller is brought in to look at my hands and absolutely refuses to say anything about what she sees there.

Mr Billy Green (as I shall call him) is the last straw. He is quite old and absolutely mad. He tells me all about how he sits on the Bluff and looks out over the ocean at the beautiful girls in Honolulu. He draws a big chalk circle on my floor with mystic symbols all around it, in which I stand while he casts out the devil. I am also quite convinced that possession by the devil must be what is wrong with me.

He throws holy water all over my pictures, regardless of whether the paint is dry or not. He ends up (after many weeks of this) with the brilliant idea that if I lie flat on my back on my bed, with him lying flat on his face on top of me, the devil will come out of my insides and possess him instead.

I really think he meant this well, and so, not wishing to hurt his feelings, ask Papa if he can please get rid of Mr Green as kindly as he can before he, or I, lose control altogether. And that was (temporarily) the end of the quacks.

During most of the time at this place, I have been most uncomfortably aware of a peculiar and unaccountable smell around me. No one else can smell it.

Thinking it must be something to do with the devil, I fear it very much. In the corner of my room, just out of sight but always there,

111

lies a great big buffalo. It is brown and blue, and stays there quietly all the time to look after me. I sing to it and about it, and my friends know it is there.

I have painted a picture (all at once, in one day) of a big, blue Negro beating a drum. He hangs there on the wall, beating his drum very loud, mocking me and waiting for the devil to come and swallow me up altogether.

At this time I weigh only 75lbs and give myself a fright looking in the mirror. I see that the cross I cut on my forehead soon after I went back to Wolf has now faded almost right away.

So now I cut it again, as deep as I can, since it is there to keep the devil away from me. I cut off the bit of hair that hangs over it to stop people asking questions. I shine up the cross which hangs around my neck, and the other one on my ring, which Wolf gave me soon after we first met, for the same purpose. Since I did take these precautions I suppose I must have still been caring what would happen to me. Or maybe I was just scared.

Chapter Eleven

One evening now Stuart Campbell, whom I much respect and like, is telling me a story which involves the gesture of a child offering something in one outstretched hand.

I want to paint this, and so kneel on the floor in front of the long mirror in my room, making the same gesture with my hand. What I see here is myself not offering but asking for something that I want so very much but know that I can never have. I do not know what it is I want so much. I become most terribly sick, and lie there on the floor for a long time absolutely stiff with fright.

Another evening, Stuart is with me and I ask him what he thinks is wrong with my pictures, because I know something is. He looks at all the pictures in my room for a long time and then tells me: 'You need to fall in love.' I think I do see what he means by this and that he is most likely right.

It is very soon after this that I meet Leo, wish to fall in love with him and most certainly think I have. The first time I notice Leo, he is sitting beside me at some party, holding my hand and saying we should get out of here and go somewhere quieter to talk.

We go to some hotel veranda where he asks me why I look so sad. I tell him why – so far as I know it – and presently notice he is actually in tears about my troubles and truly caring very much. So, are you coming home with me tonight, Leo? Yes. I did not expect this simple answer since he is different to my usual friends.

He is a very gentle, tender-hearted person, appears to be all in one piece, and just about everything in the world I am most wishing someone would be. That night I really think that all my problems are about to fade away. I expect I cried for once with happiness, while Leo must have cried from grief.

I don't know what we do the next day, but by the evening I can see that Leo is very upset indeed. Why? Because his wife is such a lovely person that he will not be able to bear hurting her. She is in Johannesburg seeing some counsellor about the problems of their marriage. She may or may not come back but most likely will. He cannot bear to hurt me either, but we both know it is already far too late to prevent everyone concerned from being very badly hurt indeed.

I do not remember much of what happens next and some of it is hearsay. Leo's wife comes back almost at once, he tells her exactly what has happened, and they go on trying to overcome their problems together, with the help of psychologist Ronald Albino, who is their close friend.

During the day, Leo is trying to get on with his work in my room or taking me around with him wherever he has to go. At night, I lie on my bed listening to my drummer banging away on the wall, knowing that I have hurt far too many people already in my life. Knowing that Leo and his wife are both doing everything they can to help me, but there is nothing anyone can do except myself.

One evening now the drummer speaks to me (this sounds most like the loud echo of a voice), saying that the whole world belongs to the devil and I must go off now and look for him. But first I must tear up all my books, smash up everything in my room and kill my cat.

Hearing the terrible noise I am making doing these things, Mama comes over from the house. I take her by the throat at once and try my best to strangle her to death. Had I not been in such a weak state and had she not been a very strong woman, my life would have come to an end soon after this, I suppose.

But she gets away from me in time and runs screaming into the house. My head is very clear now and I walk calmly out into the road and take a bus down to the beach, which is where I expect and hope to meet the devil. I am feeling very strong now, and run up and down the beach between Addington and Blue Lagoon, about 18 miles altogether, that night.

I am talking to someone in the fairground, asking: 'Faith in what?' I am down by the sea, remembering Oscar Wilde's story about the fisherman who stood with his back to the moon and cut his shadow away from his feet, because it was his soul and he had to get rid of it.

I find a stick and try to do the same thing for myself. I keep on running into the sea, and always, some distance in front of me are two black figures, coming towards me but never getting any closer. I know these are what I came to find, but however fast I run I can't get any nearer to them.

Presently I hear the sirens of police cars going up and down the road as the police search for me, and I lie flat in the bushes when they come too close. Sometime towards the end of the night, I am about to give up my search for the devil on the beach, since he must have gone away. But I see a light in the window of a flat I know belongs to Gerry Strauss, who I know he will not ask me any questions.

I am just about to run into the building when I see my own car coming slowly towards me. In it are Timothy, Wendy, Julian and Leo. Timothy was sure that I would be somewhere on the beach and has been up and down here all the night.

I run away around the back of the building but, since I fall, they catch me. They take me up to Gerry's flat, where he is having one of his usual parties and is unsurprised to see us all. I am lying on the floor there, very cold, very wet and covered with sand, talking to someone.

Later on, I am at home again and someone else is cleaning me up in the bath. Dr Jackson, who I much dislike, is there in my room, looking helpless, stupid and cross as usual. The whole room is full of people, all looking upset. I now say that, since I am a danger to everyone I know, I want to be shut up somewhere now, once and for good.

So that morning I am taken to a psychiatrist called Dr Archer, who says I must go at once to Fort Napier mental hospital, at Pietermaritzburg. Timothy takes me there in his car, with my parents following in theirs.

I remember a bit of the drive, talking to Timothy. I remember arriving there that night. I am in a dim little room, where some man is trying to make me sign some things on a form I do not want to write. Papa is arguing with him, and finally I write out that I will have as many electric shocks as anyone likes – I expect I remembered Dr Lambert saying these are a good thing. I will also stay here as long as anyone would like.

So now I sit on a bed behind a screen, with my suitcase which contains two bottles of brandy, many boxes of various pills and nothing much else. I think I had better fortify myself with brandy, and offer it to passers-by who look as if they need it too, until the night nurse comes and takes the case and everything in it away for good.

She takes me to a room full of people in bed, dresses me up in some sort of shirt, and leaves me alone for the rest of the night. The lights are always on all night here. Everyone makes a lot of noise. The windows are barred, the doors are always locked. Very well then. I can do no damage here.

The A Ward of Fort Napier is three sides of filthy, old buildings, with a square of earth in the middle and a fence all round the whole lot. One side has a room full of women who cannot move about, and a row of locked cells with a hole in each door so you can see what is lying about on the mattress or the floor, or crawling about in there.

Another side has the nurses' room and a big room full of trolleys where people lie to have their shocks, howling and screaming most horribly when this happens. There is a recreation room, which can only be got into by finding a nurse who may be willing to take you there and lock you up again inside. There is a bathroom, which you can only use by finding a nurse who may be willing to let you have the tap, and lock you inside. The only nurse who is willing to do anything like this is only here at night.

The bath I am supposed to use is in the corridor at the end of my ward, along with the lavatory which has no door and is in no state for any human to use, any more than the bath is. We each have a plate and a spoon for eating, but these are so revolting that I will not eat at all. In fact, this is all a great deal worse than I expected and worse than I am saying here.

I am sitting in the nurses' room trying to answer questions from Dr Ginsburg, but crying now so much I can't say anything at all and knowing there is nothing I can possibly explain. Dr Ginsburg gives up trying to make me say anything and tells me that I am to have insulin shocks at once and may not write a letter, telephone, or see anyone I know for the next two weeks at least.

I remember the awful skeleton at Mill Hill, lying there in the dark, being filled up day and night with mountains of greasy, grey potatoes. So when they are about to give me insulin, I drink from the hot water bottle which is there to keep me warm, because I know if I drink anything at all they cannot give me insulin. That's what they said, anyway, and it must be true because – after endless shouting at me – I get electric shocks instead.

Since I will not eat, I am allowed one visitor, once, who is a friend of Dr Ginsburg and known to my father. She brings me a sack full of oranges, a wooden plate and a beautiful silver spoon, which my father has sent to me. I keep these in my bed and wash myself when I can.

I see Timothy climbing up the fence and jumping down inside, running across to find me. But he is caught and is never let in to see me. I stay there about two months altogether, either dazed from electric shocks or demented by general shocks in more lucid moments.

Presently my parents are allowed to take me out twice every week into the town. I do not know who they are and ask them only for a bath, which I have every time they come, in the Plough Hotel. Mama later says this is all very difficult because I am very wild indeed at this time, very hostile to everyone, and making much disturbance in the hospital as well. Eventually I sit at a table with many doctors, all asking me questions, which I don't remember if I answer or not.

Dr Ginsburg concludes there is something wrong with my brain and I should go to Sterkfontein mental hospital to see what this might be. She thinks the shocks have improved me in some ways but staying here is doing me more harm than good. Therefore I can go home now for a while, but only if someone is with me all the time, every night and day.

My parents say I asked for Wendy then, saying she is the only person I can bear anywhere near me. She comes straight back from Johannesburg, leaving her new job there to look after me.

They tell me that when Leo came to see me as soon as I got home, I asked him who he was and what he wanted. I did not know my parents either, or remember seeing anyone I recognized at all except for Wendy, whom I sometimes knew was there. They say that Leo came back often, but I never knew him. When in later years I see him, I never do feel anything at all about him. So what was all that about? I would really like to know.

The first person who comes into focus with sudden and absolute clarity is Selby. This is not surprising since he is a truly sensational person in every sort of way.

He is sitting on my bed reading a poem he has written about me. I do not understand the poem but am listening to his heart beating quietly under my ear, and I notice the drummer on the wall is now silent and meaningless. Perhaps it was this that woke me up just at this moment.

117

Selby explains his poem and talks about what he thinks of life in general. Presently he says he ought to be at a party but does not want to go since it is 'political' and bound to be gloomy. But, if I like, we can show up for a little while.

He gets his seven-foot-something frame into his little green car with me beside him, and we set off for the flat of Harold Strachan [a leader of the ANC's armed struggle against apartheid]. I remember asking Selby why we are going along all these dark, little lanes, and he says (in a Deep South accent, which means he is serious): 'Honey, have you no idea what happens if this car gets stopped by the police?'

Well, I suppose I have, but South Africa's race laws stretch my imagination beyond its limit and I never take any notice of them. Understandable. But if there are cops around Strachan's place, I shall have to say he is my chauffeur! Our sense of humour much restored by this idea, we finally arrive. If there are cops around, they do not stop us here.

This party is indeed 'political' and gloomy. The gloomy girl beside me goes on and on at me, and I wish Selby would hurry up and stop trying to cheer things up and take me home again before I fall asleep.

Looking around for refuge, I see a young man across the room who appears to be much more interested in me than who is going to blow up what, when and how and so on. He looks to me like an El Greco figure, with his great, big, mournful eyes.

He tells me he lives in Johannesburg and would like to be of help to me when I arrive up there. He writes out his address for me, and his name, which is Andre Gialerakis.

He tells me much later that I appeared perfectly reasonable that evening and that he made up his mind I was 'the woman in his life' in the moment I came through the door with Selby. In fact, I remember very little about this meeting, being very tired and confused.

Soon after this, Selby goes off to teach at Princeton University in America, where he is killed, most improbably, in a motor accident. I often wonder if he has been a victim of assassination.

Wendy has gone back to Johannesburg, since I shall soon be there and am quiet enough to be left without a 'keeper'. She is now most terribly upset about being the way she is and trying not to be.

I have a copy made for her of the silver cross that hangs around my neck and take this to the Catholic Cathedral, to look for a priest who will give it a blessing. I suppose this would make it more likely to chase the devil away from Wendy. The priest I find is unaccountably unwilling to do any such thing and clearly thinks I should still be in Fort Napier. I relate this incident to show that I was still much preoccupied with these sort of thoughts.

Timothy has found a job in Johannesburg as well and is going to take Mama and me there in his car, since no one else feels either able or willing to take responsibility for me on the way. I believe they expect me to jump out of the car and run away.

I do not know at all what is going to happen to me and say I want to be shut up in Sterkfontein. My head is far from clear and I am positively crippled with pains, which no one can think what to do about.

Papa has a friend in Johannesburg called Mrs Lean, who visits us sometimes. She is a very weird and forceful lady, who gazes at me most intently, mostly seeing wings all around me. She now states that she – with the help of her yogi and her doctor, Brown (as I shall call him) – will fix me up altogether when I get to Johannesburg. Thus saving me from Sterkfontein, of which prospect she and Papa do not approve.

The drive to Johannesburg, Mrs Lean, Dr Brown and most likely Sterkfontein is all very hazy. I expect I stunned myself as best I could with every kind of painkiller available, for every kind of pain, before we started off. My pessimism here is unfounded since I am quite soon now going to have about the best time I ever did have in my life.

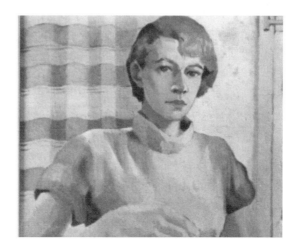

Hilary, a self portrait

Title unknown, late 60s

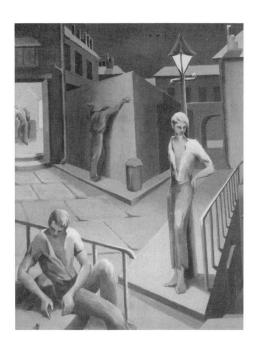

Left: Two paintings from
Hilary's Street Scenes
series, circa 1956

Andre and Hilary

Alan Paton (*Left*) opening Hilary's exhibition at the International Club in 1955. It was the only venue in Durban at the time when people of all races were legally allowed to meet

Andre, broadcasting at the SABC as Philip Armitage

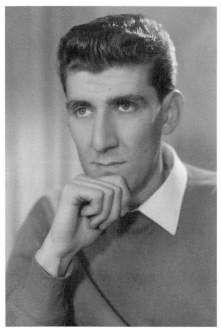

Andre Gialerakis

Hilary and Andre signing the marriage register
watched by Julian, Felicity, Eileen, family friend and
Leslie Grant

Hilary and Andre 'honeymooning'
on the Edinburgh Castle on their way
to England

Hilary

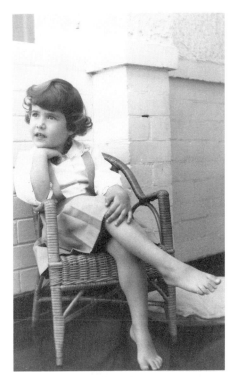

Antonia

Antonia, 1972

Hilary with Antonia

Hilary with Eileen and some of her later paintings

Chapter Twelve

The 18 months or so I spend in Hillbrow start off rather badly. Mama and I are in a sordid room, in a sordid hotel, somewhere in Johannesburg, where I mostly stay in bed.

Mrs Lean – at her home – sees all sorts of visions round me, tells me when and where to attend her yoga classes, and produces her doctor, V, who starts to fill me up with many useless pills. I do not like any part of this and telephone the young man I met at Harold Strachan's party, who said that he would help me here.

Andre comes over in the evening and Mama leaves him in the room where I lie in bed. I am still very hazy here, but remember that he takes off most of his clothes, spends some time talking and then gets up, dresses and goes home. Well, he kisses me goodnight very nicely, is as helpful as he can be and I look forward to seeing him again.

We stay in this hotel for about three days, Dr Brown visits me here and then we move to a 'chrome and glass' sort of hotel in Hillbrow. Andre comes here to make polite conversation with Mama and take me for drives around Johannesburg. One evening, sitting in his car beside the lake, Andre asks me how old I think he is. I have no idea at all – have simply never wondered – but am surprised when he says that he is only 23.

I am also disconcerted, because he sounds as if his age is somehow unfortunate and I ought to know why. I don't know what to say about this, and think I say that he does not seem any particular sort of age to me, and leave it at that.

I am soon fed up with Mrs Lean's fat ladies trying to stand on their heads; fed up with Dr Brown's pills doing me no good at all; and worse than fed up with having to live in the same room with Mama. However, I do like Hillbrow and now intend to find a room for myself there and try to do whatever I can about myself to avoid Sterkfontein, if possible.

I find a big, empty room at the Montparnasse Restaurant Coffee Bar in Kotze Street, where there are about six such rooms and mine looks exactly what I want. My pictures and other things arrive from Durban, Mama moves into the Chelsea Hotel nearby, and I settle down here in my room to try to put my life together somehow.

Dr Brown, a round blob on top of a larger round, white blob, all done up in some sort of raincoat and hat, comes to see me in the afternoon and finds me lying on my bed absolutely doubled up with pain. He gets on to the bed with me, pulls me onto his lap, puts his hand right down the front of my pants and tells me that what I need is to relax, and that he is showing me the best way for me to do so.

I can see by the horrible look on his horrible face that he does not even think he means this well. Why I don't just hit these types I simply can't imagine, but I never do, right up to this day. In this case, instant floods of hopeless tears must put him off and he soon gives up and goes away.

But – having recovered somewhat – I am now feeling very, very angry about absolutely everything. I tell Mama exactly what happened (her sensibilities, unlike those of Papa, are absolutely shockproof) and that she should go and tell Mrs Lean all about her Dr Brown, neither of whom I ever wish to see again.

So now I return to ordinary painkillers and brandy, try to pull myself together in this way, and direct my thoughts back to my paintings, which are hanging all around me on the walls. Timothy and Wendy spend most of their free time with me and in the evenings we sit in the coffee bar downstairs playing endless games of cards.

We play here so constantly that one night Alex Carvallos, the Greek owner of this place, sends us over a whole new set of cards and we become good friends. I like this place very much indeed, and am happy in the evenings here, watching the colourful Hillbrow scene going on around me from the safety of my seat against the wall, with my trusted friends beside me.

But in the daytime, alone in my room, afraid to go out even to sit in the coffee bar downstairs by myself, I am very frightened and very lonely. I hear the drummer in the painting on the wall all the time. My buffalo has come back, which is some help but not enough. This room is very big and dark, and I walk round and round in it thinking I shall have to go to Sterkfontein after all.

Andre comes to visit me quite often. We are getting to know each other a bit better, though this is something of a struggle. I have never been able to contend with the rigmarole one is generally supposed to go through before actually saying, doing, or being anything of much importance with someone that I want to know, who wants to know me too. I think it is pointless and confusing. It makes me very nervous.

Andre does not feel like this and so at this time we seldom say, or do, or be anything of much importance together. I often wonder why he visits me at all. When he is with me in the evenings, Andre sits up talking until it is so late, I really have to go to sleep.

While he sits in a chair watching me, I go to bed, presuming that since he is still there he means to join me for one reason or another. But he does not. He just sits on in the chair while I try to go to sleep.

I am more than somewhat disenchanted with the whole idea of love, but all the same, I wish and ask that Andre will come and lie here with me. So that I can go to sleep and stop being so frightened for a little while at least. I don't know how many nights it is that Andre sits with me like this, but since he does not come here often it must be quite a few.

He does eventually, for no apparent reason, get out of his chair one night, come into my bed and make love to me, and stay a little while to let me rest. But he always goes home to his sister's house before two o' clock, so that she will not ask what he has been doing out so late.

I resent this very much and resent the many evenings when he does not come at all because he is looking after Athena's children while she and her husband are out. It is either that, or political meetings, neither of which seems important enough if he really cares about me much at all. I presume that he does not, but am beginning to wish he would, since, although I do not wish to love him, I am now sure I either do or shall.

My feeling about all this is that I am in the sea, struggling not to drown, while a lifesaver nearby treads water calmly, watching me with academic interest to see if I do actually drown or not. I am upset by never knowing if or when Andre may turn up nor having any idea at all what he thinks or feels about me or why he will not make himself clear about any of this. Well, he won't, and all this waiting and wondering is an added strain which is too much for me altogether. Andre says much later that nearly all the time I was in Hillbrow I was very wild indeed, had endless hallucinations and threw myself about almost violently in bed, even when asleep.

One evening, I pour a pan of boiling oil all over my foot, with the idea that the physical pain this will cause will be so acute I shall not be able to think about anything else at all. It does not hurt so much at once, but soon my whole foot has blown up into one enormous blister and my leg is blowing up as well. It is getting bigger and bigger every minute and the pain now is so acute, I could not wish for more.

So I lie down watching it and feeling pain and nothing else until I have to get up, find I can't stand on this foot and it is all going black. This is more than I intended and, fearing that my foot is going to burn itself away, I telephone Andre.

I explain that I have burnt myself and ask if Athena's husband, who is a doctor, can please come and do something about it. So Andre arrives, looks at what used to be my foot and takes me to the general hospital. I don't remember anything about this, except for having a vision of Alan Paton there, dressed up as a doctor.

I don't remember anything else much for some time except the difficulties of moving around on one leg. Andre believes to this day that I burnt myself like this simply to make him feel sorry for me. My belief is that basic instincts would prevent anyone in their right mind being able to do it at all, let alone for a silly reason.

Andre's brother-in-law John dresses my foot at his house. I remember him saying that all the tendons will probably shrink up and die but, although shrunk, they do not appear to be dead yet.

I suppose this is where I first meet Athena, John and their children. Now Andre sometimes takes me there in the evenings to stay with him and mind the children. One evening we oversleep on the sofa in front of the fire and wake up to see Athena and John looking at us in such a way that I never want to go back there again. I begin to understand just how much Andre's family disapprove of him seeing me at all.

One evening I am in my room talking to Timothy, telling him that I truly do love Andre and that I hope to stay with him and try to live a different sort of life. This is a most painful moment, which I remember very clearly. Timothy knows I really mean it this time, says nothing very much, goes away back to Durban, and writes me beautiful letters full of love and understanding for a long time afterwards.

Mama goes home, presumably believing that Andre (who inspires confidence, even at 23) will look after me and I won't have to go to Sterkfontein after all. Andre has left his sister's home and got a very nice flat for himself now in Hillbrow. I move out of the big, dark room into a small, sunny one along the passage, where I settle down to paint and enjoy life very much indeed.

I think I should say here that no one – doctor, psychiatrist or anyone else – ever suggested that I might be drinking too much, until I came to the conclusion myself when Antonia was about two years' old. Also, that I only had sedatives at brief intervals until about that time.

Chapter Thirteen

In the sunny little room over the Café Montparnasse, I altogether lose my usual feeling of being someone who is trying to balance staying still in an alien world which goes round and round without me, under my feet. I find instead a context in which I can now live and enjoy my life, going around with a satisfactory sort of world that does not want to throw me off.

I still have many pains that will not go away but I feel safe and happy enough to be able to direct my thoughts away from these, most of the time at least. I get up early in the morning and paint here every day until I am too tired to go on. If I want a short rest, I go downstairs and drink coffee with Alex or his girlfriend Babs, or sit at one of the tables in the street outside to watch the passers-by.

While I am painting, there are often people in the room with me, many of whom are Wendy's friends. They tell me all about their lives in the 'gay society' of Hillbrow. This is really startling and goes on to a considerable extent in some of the other rooms up here. Impala (also known as Mrs A), for instance, is a very wild girl indeed, whose whole room – and mind – is occupied by the biggest bed that I have ever seen in my life. Impala, Wendy and various boys and girls rush between this room and mine, describing each other's awful infidelities with such drama and evident enjoyment that I enjoy it too. I am gratified to find them hanging onto my words of wisdom, greatly admiring my paintings and treating me with absolute consideration.

When I come to a difficult bit of painting or simply want to be alone, I shut my door, with a suitable notice outside, and no one is offended by this or ever disturbs me by knocking on the door.

I have always believed, and said, that it is quite impossible for anyone to be a creative artist of any sort and live an unselfish life at the same time. I can't think of any at all that did manage this and no one I can ask, either. Having finished my painting for the day, I relax myself with enough brandy to go straight to sleep until about six o' clock, when I wake up refreshed and ready to enjoy the evening.

Andre is teaching at Marist Brothers prep school, where he went as a child. He turns up after work and we sit here and talk to each other, and to people coming in and out for drinks, advice, comfort or just for company. If Andre is surprised by my companions and our way of life – I suppose he must be – he never shows it. So they soon accept him, to a considerable degree at least.

He helps us all out by providing a steady supply of gin for the dear old lady who is supposed to keep order up here. She is thus in a suitably euphoric state to enjoy our antics and can be heard snoring peacefully before anything she might feel obliged to protest about is likely to happen.

Alex downstairs knows all about Andre's family, who are much-respected members of the Greek community in Johannesburg, and he is honoured by his presence at the Montparnasse. So there is a table permanently reserved for our dinner in the restaurant, on the balcony inside where we can watch the dancing, listen to the band and entertain whoever we like until closing time around one o' clock.

Andre loves to dance. He does so with so much grace that I am enchanted watching him there with various girls we know, or with Alex and other Greek men who do their own traditional Greek dancing and singing together towards closing time, when the musicians are really going wild as well.

Presently Andre's friends come to join us at our table too. Some are Greeks (some sent by Athena to see what her little brother is up to with wicked me) and one of these I do like very much indeed.

Johnny Carados is a very quiet, gentle boy, with soft blond hair and soft blue eyes, and no ambition to own a fleet of tankers or any such thing his family expect of him. I really do love Johnny so much that Andre only tells me recently how he finished his life in a room filled with gas many years ago.

Andre has another friend, Patrick Levy, who is a magician (Inner Circle and very serious about it). He sits with us, pulling lighted cigarettes out of the air, tearing up hankies in half right in front of our eyes and then reproducing them intact and so on, endlessly. He is quite indisputably 'magic' and great fun always.

Andre also has friends I do not like at all. These are young men who were at University with him and seem to me to have never left it. They don't, either: they nearly all have gone back there to lecture.

These I find always rude, uncouth and generally hostile towards me. They sit and mutter pompous, pretentious, 'political' talk at Andre, while I wonder how or why he puts up with them. They are types we both come to call 'unwashed bachelors', although some do now have wives to whom they are just as rude and inconsiderate as ever. In fact, they are the sort of men who really don't like women. I do not understand, like or want to know them.

Fortunately they mostly live in Durban and soon go back to lurk about in squalid backrooms there, patronising their various black 'friends' in the most embarrassing way they possibly can. This diatribe is because they are all going to come back into my life in about two years' time and drive me into an absolute frenzy of anxiety and irritation.

Andre at this time has an air of very smooth sophistication. He is always elegant, immaculate, polite. He has the absolutely unmistakeable look of someone who likes women very much indeed.

What he actually knows about them is something I have never been able to find out, since he is still evasive or contradicting himself every time I ask him anything of this sort. Anyway, he spends all of every night with me now and only goes away in time to get to school.

Demonstrating – more or less from habit – various reasonably respectable bedroom tricks learned by me long before I was ever 23, I see that Andre is not only impressed but most surprised. This should have told me a lot about a whole lot of things about him, I suppose, but of course it did not. I am surprised by his surprise, pleased by his evident pleasure, but do not propose to go any further along these lines in case he suddenly sends me up the wall by turning into someone completely different, like so many people do.

He has not done this yet and so I sleep in peace with him, believing that he probably does love me, wondering why he just can't say so, and hoping that my life is going to stay put like this, if not get better still. It occurs to me here that in fact optimism has caused me a great deal more trouble in my life than pessimism ever did.

About this time, my parents write to say that I should visit them in Durban. The perpetually nomadic state of my life has given me the most acute aversion to moving at all from any one place to another, even for a few days, and I do not wish to go. But for some reason I feel

I have to do this now. Andre indicates that if I go and see my parents for a week, then he will come and join me for another week in some hotel, and take me home again in his car.

My parents are staying (temporarily of course) in someone else's house in Innes Road. I am overcome by pain as soon as I get there, feel totally disorientated all over again, and most unhappy all the time I am there.

After a week, I arrive at the Fairydene Hotel, in Sarnia, which is suitably deserted and remote. I sit up until late that night, wondering if Andre is going to turn up or not. Knowing that his most extreme aversion is to committing himself in any way whatever, I doubt if he will come at all. But eventually the door opens, there he is, and I experience the most rare delight of finding the right thing happening at the right moment, just the way I want it to.

During this next week, Andre shows me a very different side to his nature. He is considerate and affectionate to me, wears comfortable old clothes, drops the deadpan look as much as he can, plays about on the beach and is positively human. I am startled when he makes love to me in an almost non-existent shelter on a beach littered with people, quite regardless of what they saw or thought of him.

This was really the most uncharacteristic thing I have ever known Andre to do, since he is positively afflicted with concern about public image. I now suppose that being away from Athena's atmospherics and the whole conservative Greek community must have gone to his head. It was during this pleasant holiday that I committed myself entirely to Andre and thought about actually staying with him for good.

Back in Hillbrow, I move my easel to Andre's flat and paint there in the mornings. I am painting a picture for him, showing myself offering my love to him, which turns out very well indeed. The rest of the time we spend as before, at the Montparnasse, where we are safe from actual invasion by Andre's relatives.

I believe they would not like to come here because Alex discarded his Greek wife for an English Babs, has a disreputable pool room downstairs, our den of vice upstairs and an unashamedly lesbian daughter. In fact, Alex and Babs are two of the nicest, most devoted people I ever knew.

Sitting in the car outside one day, I see a very wild woman rushing across the road at me. She is clawing at my face through the window, shrieking away in Greek. Andre dashes out of the café and removes Aunt Mary with much noise and difficulty.

One morning I see Aunts Mariora and Ephigenia advancing down the passage to Andre's flat. I lock the door and jump off the terrace wall into the street, and run home as fast as I can. I have mixed feelings about all this. I see that Andre is having a hard time with all these people, but I see also that he is standing up to them, refusing to be bullied and made a fool of, and making up his mind to be free of the whole lot. This being as difficult as it must be for him, it must mean that he does love me and wants to keep me with him, although he can't quite bring himself to say so.

One day Andre and I are lying on the grass beside the lake, talking about our future. He has never been outside of South Africa, wants to go off and see Europe, and proposes to do this now.

He says when he has finished seeing Europe and settled down somewhere there, he will send for me to come and join him. Hearing this, I think Andre cannot be serious. I know that he has never believed or accepted that there is anything much the matter with me. But how can he possibly suppose that I could just be left like this, to wait around in Africa for an indefinite time, with an indefinite future, without getting into trouble and coming unstuck altogether, defeats me altogether.

I don't think there would even be pieces left to pick up and I try to make him understand this now. Andre is silent, disapproving and put out, while I tell him that the events of my whole life have proved quite clearly what I am trying to explain. I watch Andre struggling to convert unacceptable, inconvenient but indisputable facts (about which Mama has told him a good deal already) into something that will fit his own opinion. Which is, that I could perfectly well manage every aspect of my life without any help at all if I really wanted to, and most likely always could.

I remember endless letters from my father, left usually under my door, saying that I am by far the most sensible person he knows. Saying much about my unbeatable guardian angels, who are certain to keep any sort of harm away from me. Saying all these sort of things right in the middle of the very worst times in my life.

I know that Papa could not bear his life, or mine, without such beliefs. I hope he truly does manage to convince himself and I do not mind this from my father. But Andre is a very different matter. Can he really believe that everything I ever did was just for willful, malicious, enjoyable amusement – that I simply talked my way into such places as Mill Hill or Fort Napier for entertainment, fooling every psychiatrist I ever saw into finally wanting to have me actually certified insane?

I do not remember how my conversation with Andre ends, but it is repeated one way or another over and over again for the next five months, coming to no sort of conclusion for me.

Looking at all the pictures on my walls, right up to the ceiling, I think that I will have another exhibition now and propose to really enjoy it this time.

Most exhibitions I have seen in the usual sort of galleries are boring, unprofitable, and half empty – the other half being ladies showing more interest in each other's hats that the surrounding pictures. So I will have mine here, at the Montparnasse, where people will be sitting down to eat and drink and so likely to really notice what is on the walls.

Alex is delighted with the prospect of more customers and extra publicity. He will not hear of any payment, but insists on providing coffee and so on for the opening occasion. So I must be sure that the publicity is good.

Here Mrs Lean finally serves a very useful purpose indeed by producing Adam Leslie and his wife Judith Gluckman, who is a well-known and very good painter. Adam is going to open the show in his usual amusing manner and Judith (who makes most gratifying remarks about my pictures) tells me what to do best about the critics and so on.

She and Mrs Lean between them produce a list of 1,000 people it would be a good idea to invite, and a printer who will make the invitations. I now take photos of my paintings round to the newspaper critics, making sure that I shall recognize them and say the right things to them when they turn up. Judith says, quite rightly, that this is essential to success.

Practically everyone I know comes up to help address and send off my thousand invitations. Timothy, who has appeared periodically to make sure my improbable Greek lover is turning out all right, arrives to help, support and keep an eye on me.

Parents, Felicity and Julian arrive as well. Julian – now gigantic – is a great help with Andre and Timothy, hanging up paintings all over the whole place, which has to be done carefully but in a hurry.

Papa, with a whole variety of cameras, is taking pictures of everything and everyone in sight, muttering about 'clouds of glory' as usual. I hope he is not going to burst into tears at the wrong moment, as he often does when overexcited.

With all this support and gaiety, I feel reasonably confident that I shall not lose my head, even if I had time to. Mighty Mouse is at last telling everyone else how things ought to be done and much enjoying this experience!

Mama and my sister, done up like two Christmas trees, are asking anxiously: 'What are you going to wear?' Well, I am going to wear just what I always do, which is black pants and a jersey. I have asked Adam and my friends not to alter their usual appearance in any way. Papa has brought his orange corduroy jacket, which I gave him long ago to cheer him up.

By five o' clock, the whole place is full up and by half past five there is a long queue outside in the street. I really believe those thousand people did turn up, one day or another, so Alex got all the publicity and custom he needed.

Adam and I are standing alone on the balcony and he starts up with his speech, which begins in his usual amusing manner but ends up very serious, being the person that he really is. This nearly makes me lose my head after all, but I do manage to say what I have to say: just thank you to him and everyone who is here.

The pianist starts up again, although drowned out by general gaiety and rioting. Here once more is exactly the right thing happening in just the way I want it to. At this time, I think I have all I ever wanted in my life.

For the next few weeks, I spend most of the time downstairs attending to people who are interested in my pictures. I have much amusement inventing answers to the usual question, which is: 'What does it mean?' I answer according to what sort of person it is who is asking.

Some actually ask for 'something to go with their curtains' and are easily led to the pictures which I think the least well of. Some I see admiring and wanting a picture (usually one of the best), but are not likely to ask because they can't afford it. Some could clearly pay anything but they must be avoided because they will always want to bargain, whatever the price may be.

I keep different lists in Alex's desk, produce whichever one I think will be best, learn quite a lot about some aspects of human nature and get rid of most of my pictures.

When there are only a few left, Wendy brings some of hers to be put up with them. Later, I put what I have left in a small exhibition at Springs. What remains after this, I pack up and send to my parents to keep in Durban.

So now there are no pictures left in my room. I stop painting altogether and memories of the next four or five months are very hazy indeed. It seems that my kaleidoscope of life is given another little twist here and all the fragments which are me, although all the same of course, fall back into the wrong sort of pattern.

I remember two American professors who want to buy my picture of some refugees. They stay around the Montparnasse, waiting for money to be sent to pay for it and talk a lot about the splendid life everyone is having in South Africa. So I say to Andre that we should take them to Sophiatown one night to straighten their ideas on this subject, since they are very young.

I arrange this with a young black woman I know, who takes us all to visit the journalist Can Themba and another called Lewis Nkosi, in Sophiatown.

It is a very dark night. There are bodies lying around in a stupor outside of the house we visit, where Can excels himself, showing much delight in his shebeen. He sits on the remains of his sofa, clutching the lady professor close to him and overpowering her with alcohol fumes and much instructive information. There are dozens of people here in the smoky candlelight and both professors are absolutely terrified.

In Lewis's shack nearby there are two iron beds and nothing much else. Lewis is very articulate and very angry (Sophiatown was being demolished by the apartheid government at the time). Most people here are smoking dagga (marijuana), drinking beer and making the true state of their lives very clear, even to the American professors. They later buy my picture and thank me most profusely for this whole experience, though I doubt the lady professor will ever really get over it.

I remember parties at the house of Alistair Mundy-Castle. He is a professor, I suppose, and turns out to be the man who made the special brain machine that was supposed to be used on me in Sterkfontein. He is also a most brilliant abstract painter and I like him very much indeed.

These parties were very wild, since Mundy's wife has a passion for 'Hell's Angels' boys, who turn up in droves and make lots of noise. I spend a lot of time with Mundy elsewhere, talking about most interesting things, until he goes off to Russia for scientific research, saying he will bring me back a polar bear and some new ideas about his brain box.

I remember taking Wendy to a very nice lady psychiatrist, who tells her that she really is a true lesbian and should concentrate on how best to live with this condition. Wendy took her advice and went off to live on a Greek island with a Greek girl, where she still is.

I remember one morning at Montparnasse, when Babs comes over to warn me that one of Andre's relatives is sitting there watching me. This is a nice-looking young woman and I go straight to her table, sit down and ask if she has something she wants to say to me.

Andre's cousine Cissy says she wants very much to say how very sorry she is and ashamed she is about the way they all behave to me. We talk a long time and she is very nice to me indeed – and remains so right up until the time she and her husband, Phelon, are killed in a stupid motor car accident outside of Athens. Her mother, Aunt Katina, has been very good to Andre, Antonia and me ever since, and Cissy's three children, now grown up, come to visit us quite often.

I do not remember when or how I come to know that Andre has booked a single flight to London for himself and has every intention of keeping to his original plan for us both. I know that I go on trying to explain as before and still ask him to take me too, until eventually he says he will, although he does not want to.

We were both short of money and cannot afford two cabins on the boat. So he says – at the very last moment – that he will marry me in Durban on the day of our boat is due to leave so that we will have the same name on our passports and be able to share a cabin. Thinking about it when I am writing this many years later, it seems an inadequate reason.

It is February 1959. I remember giving all the things I have in my room to the young boy who cleans it every day. I remember putting my teddy bear, which has slept in my bed with me for 30 years at least, into the furnace at Andre's flat. I keep nothing except a few clothes and the picture I painted for Andre.

He enjoys the flight to Durban, since he has never flown before, but I remember nothing of what happens when we get there until the evening, when there is a party for us at our hotel, arranged by my parents and attended by Alan Paton. All I recall is a most improbable mixture of people and being aware that I have had too much too drink and am not saying or being anything much the way I ought to be.

We have a perfectly horrible night in a boiling hot hotel room and go off to the Registry Office in the morning to be married. This is predictably horrible as well, although at least I am not drunk.

Later, we get on board the mail boat, where I find the cabin full of flowers from Cissy, hang up Andre's picture on the wall, and realize – in these all-too-familiar surroundings – just where I am and what I am on my way to now.

Andre said one day last week that I only married him for my self-preservation, but with these memories it seems to me this is one of the basic instincts I most particularly lack.

Editor's Note

Hilary's historical narrative ends here. Her 'diary', which follows, picks up the story some 15 years later. Although she mentions writing about these 'missing' years, no such text has been found.

To bridge the gap, it needs to be said that Hilary and Andre arrived in England and stayed for about nine months. They saw many faces from Hilary's past. But it became clear that a life in London was not to be, for either of them. They returned to Durban and, in July 1961, I was born.

They moved to a new house overlooking the beach in Umhlanga Rocks, north of Durban, where Hilary continued to paint.

Part 2: DIARY
Chapter Fourteen

It is now December 1974. I am getting more and more angry every day. I don't know why or what about really, and I don't remember ever feeling like this before.

Andre and Antonia both remark on it, so I can see it is really unusual. At first I think it may be because I feel I don't have enough consideration in my home, especially for my various efforts in trying to get well.

I think that no matter what I can achieve, it will not be enough since I am virtually required to be an altogether different person. I am likely to stay in the wrong forever, in these surroundings. If I go away this will be wrong too, since I would feel that I was running away from something I should try to overcome and I am sure they would feel exactly the same way about my doing that.

At Christmas, I refuse to speak to or visit my brother or my sister, or go out with Andre and Antonia. On Christmas Day, I drink some brandy. This will allow me to spend the afternoon with my mother, being the way she likes me to be. I do the same on New Year's Day. My mother is pleased with both occasions, telling me I have given her the best present I possibly could have. Some time either or before or after this, Mama leaves to go and live somewhere else.

There is a terrible heatwave in Durban now, which makes me feel really very ill and not able to think or do anything except just what I really have to. I remember being in a bad state about this time last year and suppose such heat has a bad effect on me. It must wear off soon. My eyelids are so blown up again and I can hardly see.

I am angry because of never being able to communicate with Andre properly. I ask him why he never talks to me about his own problems, as I always do about my own to him. Andre says he does not because I should not be interested.

So I ask if, in the whole of his adult life, there was anyone at all with whom he discussed his own personal problems. No, apart from one young man, for a few weeks of their friendship, there was no such person ever. He says he could have, with one or two people, but never did, apart from very reluctantly and only for my benefit – psychiatrist Dr Cheetham and counsellor Duncan Davidson.

I say this makes a very lopsided relationship between us and I feel that remarks about my not being interested enough to listen are clearly proved inadequate, if not just ridiculous.

I ask Andre if he thinks he knows what is wrong with me in general? Yes, he does know. Is it that he thinks it is basically just selfishness in me? Yes. Basically, that is it.

He is a bit hesitant about this and tries to take it back later, though without an alternative idea. He says that I entirely lack compassion. That I am cruel. That I must always bear in mind that on account of my background people make allowances for me and put up with behavior from me which they would not put up with from other people.

He says that I do not have the ability to feel 'altruistic' love. This is true, if it means what I think it does. But if that is what he has for me, then I simply cannot understand or live with it from him. I think I probably shouldn't live with anyone.

Antonia says she is terrified of me – I am like some sort of Dracula to her. She turns to our close friend and neighbour Jay Nivison for the maternal qualities that I lack. It is true, she does, although she loves me.

My conclusions are that I am not acceptable as a wife, a mother or a friend. Can I be acceptable as a painter? Since this means an even more selfish way of life for me to achieve anything worthwhile, I cannot suppose that would be acceptable to anyone at all either.

My conclusion about Andre is that he is able to love me only in spite of myself. He has always seen me as some sort of cause, to be saved by him, rather than as simply a person to love and share a life with. Most of all, I wish to love Andre more, or differently, or both, but like this I don't see how I can. I feel defeated just looking at him.

My efforts to find the roots of my difficulties with life and so hope to overcome them are causing much displeasure since the strain often does make me ill, withdrawn and more unsatisfactory than ever. In this climate of disapproval, it is very hard to live at all. Being so angry now is making me worse, although I sometimes think it may be some sort of self-preservation, without which I would now give up.

I cannot accept the idea that basic selfishness has caused the havoc of my life. I go on looking for other causes that, if proved, might then be overcome. A test on my brain has shown nothing, but I am doubtful as to how much better off I might be if I was shown to be an epileptic, since the fits I suffer do not occur often or last very long.

In January, I go to a doctor, a GP, and ask him to look for anything that might be wrong with my body, without any sort of connection to the state of my mind. He agrees to this and I have various examinations and X-rays, which all show nothing really wrong.

The doctor now wants me to see a surgeon. I don't ask why because he says that I must trust him absolutely. I say but of course, by all means – and leave his surgery in haste, wondering if ever I should go back. He has prescribed painkillers at my request, as well as Luminals and Seconals. But these all just make me feel half-witted and I soon stop taking any of them.

My conclusion is that I shall have to try to get better with the idea that it is 'all in the mind' after all, which is difficult because I don't really believe it.

I don't really believe it can get any hotter either, but it does, and sleeping sopping wet under a big fan every night has given me bronchitis, which I can't get rid of. I hear myself screaming one morning because I am waking up and have to live another day.

Andre's sister and her husband come and visit us. I don't know how to face this, but I think it turns out all right. Athena has been found to have a serious illness recently and is so doped she can hardly notice much.

A few days later, Andre's Uncle Manoli, his wife, and three others all came to visit us. Uncle Manoli was very displeased with our marriage and it is the first time he has ever agreed to see me. I know this is important to Andre. So I try again to do what I can, as well as I can, that evening.

Andre thanks me for this and says it was all right. But these visits do none of us any good.

One conversation Andre and I have starts with him saying that my whole problem with him is a matter of 'the battle of the sexes'. I can't imagine what he means by this and he does not explain it, as far as I can remember. I ask him why he thinks I am always on the defensive

147

with him, which worries me more and more. Andre says because I am most terrified of being smothered – and 'smother' is just 'mother' with an 's' in front. I agree that I do feel smothered by him but I had not seen it this way before.

Talking about this truly awful situation between us now, Andre says he 'came into this game' much later than I did and is therefore not so good at it as me. He says that is why every time I blow up one way or another, he feels much worse than I do.

I ask Andre why he doesn't talk to someone who might help him. He says he can only think of Duncan as someone whose opinions he respects enough, but that since they both have exactly the same view about absolutely everything there would be no point in their discussing them.

There are a whole lot of things I want to answer to this, but I don't because he looks so ill and harassed. I say, well, why not talk to me then and maybe we shall understand each other better? After all, here I am, why not tell me exactly what is wrong and missing in his life, what are his special aims?

Andre says he only wants to live a Christian life – and that is his whole aim. I am stunned speechless by this so uncharacteristic remark.

At some time, I tell him it seems that he is in a worse state than I am. I say this mostly to see what he will answer, which is, yes, he thinks so too. I am beginning to believe it myself and feel worried and alarmed about Andre.

Jay says he was terribly upset by seeing his relatives, which I think is true. But I am sure enough it is mostly because of me and I should go away and let him recover in peace, even it is about the worst possible time to do this, for various reasons. Antonia is just starting at a new school, the maid is away having a baby – and so on.

By now, I can see that Andre is looking more ill than ever and behaving in ways that show me he is very upset indeed. He does spend a lot of time on the beach though, while Antonia stays out of the house a lot of the time.

When she and I are alone, she talks to me a lot about her problems and her thoughts. She seems well and cheerful enough, and I tell her I am sorry to be so bad tempered and useless lately. I say she is a lovely, splendid girl with much strength of mind, and it is so nice that when

148

we fight it is all over and forgotten quickly, which is true. She never gets a grievance about this sort of thing.

Jay, to whom I talk quite a lot about my troubles, is looking ill and upset and I feel that I must stop seeing her now. I know I am upsetting her and she has many troubles of her own. Andre comes to talk to me about it one day in my room. He looks ill, but he talks to me at last about himself. I am very glad of this and feel a little bit of hope and much love for him.

At this time, I have a growing wish to destroy my pictures by painting black crosses on them, which will ruin them for good. Early one morning Andre finds me ready to start doing this in my room with the best pictures I have.

I don't know what happens next, except he says: 'Don't play games with me!' But I am not playing games, by no means, and never was. To hurt my pictures will be so much worse than killing myself, so that is what I have to do.

I go out and get brandy again. When I come back home, it seems I curse at Andre for a long time and tell him I will destroy all my pictures to make him understand. This is what he tells me later. I don't remember any of that, but I know I fell asleep and left my pictures alone.

Another day, Andre is sitting in my room looking ill – and finished. I tell him I don't want to kill myself for some reason I do not understand. I want to get better.

Andre says we are killing each other and that Antonia most likely is scarred for life. He says we shall not last another week before one of us breaks up altogether and something must be done at once.

He wants to go away himself, but I tell him Antonia would not and should not stay alone with me. He doesn't seem to take this in. I look at Andre sitting there and I know that I must go. I am killing my husband, whom I love. I am terrifying my child, whom I love. I am upsetting my friends and family so I can't even see them anymore.

The next morning, I drink some brandy once again, hoping to see what to do and to find the courage to do it. In the end, I ask my mother to phone the Marianhill Mission [which has a refuge for those who are ill, infirm or in crisis], to see if there is a room there at once for me. Presently she says yes, there is, and I can go today.

149

Andre has come in now and is dopey because he has been to the doctor to calm him down. I am a bit drunk but pack some things and get ready to go. I want to take my unfinished picture and hope to do that at least at Marianhill, where I think I may feel better.

I am frightened of what I am doing – frightened because I thought I lost the need to drink at times like this and see that I have not; frightened by the way Andre looks, standing there, shaking his head and saying it's a very wise decision. I am quite sure I don't know what I am doing at all, let alone being wise.

As we leave the house, I say I suppose that I will never come back here again. Andre says, do I propose to take the veil? In the car, I say this all seems like the Mad Hatter's tea party to me. He says yes, he is the Mad Hatter. I think I am the dormouse in the teapot, exactly.

Antonia is being splendid as ever, says the monastery looks fantastic and I shall love it here, listening to the nuns singing all the time. A nun greets us at the guest house, takes everything in at a glance, takes us to my room and then they all go away as quickly as possible.

That night, I am as frightened as I ever remember being in my life. I do not understand why any of this is happening, what is going on in my head, what I can do now. I think I ought to be in hospital and remember trying to get into Wakesleigh last week but it was fully booked.

I remember Andre saying that I might do anything at any moment and he never knows if I am going to kill myself or stick a knife into his back. I think I was angry because I knew he must know this, must have known it all along as well as I do, but has not done anything to help me, except go along with whatever I, in my desperation, may decide to do. I can't decide right by myself. If I could, how come my life has been the way it has been and still is?

The next day, I force myself to paint all morning, but I am very confused and think I shall spoil the picture, which I now don't want to do. It is very hot and dead quiet except for bells ringing and people singing in the chapel outside. I want to go there but am afraid to go out.

Everyone here creeps about looking half dead, and I think I am dead too but just can't, or won't, lie down. I sleep for hours and hours on and off all the time.

Next day when I wake up, I know that I must not go back to live with Andre and Antonia. Not for a long time anyway – and then only if I can be a proper person again and be able to stay sober.

I remember what I wrote for Duncan about the time in Hillbrow when I did manage to be all right. So I will try to find a room like that in Durban and stay there.

I can't imagine how I can live by myself now, but clearly have to do so. I wish there was someone I could talk to but there is not. The people who care for me would be upset, except for Timothy. I have asked far too much from him far too often and will not do so again.

Andre phones at breakfast time and I tell him I will go and live in a room in Durban. He will come to see me the next day and I will try to explain. I hope he will think that is all right and know it is not because I don't want to live with him.

I love Andre and Antonia as much as I can love anyone. I don't know how I can live without them but I must not hurt them anymore. Not them or anyone else, which means I must keep myself to myself.

If Duncan comes back soon, I can get to see him then and I think he will go on trying to help make me better. I can tell him everything because he can't be hurt by me. He may not be willing to give me much advice but he will not burst into tears or treat me with contempt. I have to believe this and trust Duncan as I said I would. Well I think I do. But not enough.

All of this I wrote in a book, various days since Christmas. Now at Marianhill I am writing it out again to send to Duncan, which, considering how horrible and stupid it all is, shows about as much trust as I am capable of. I write it all out today, because I don't know at all what will happen when Andre arrives tomorrow.

On Tuesday morning, Andre arrives looking ill but more composed. He tells me Dr Cohen says he has an ulcer and he is going for X-rays. Andre stays about two hours talking about various ways he might dispose of our house in Umhlanga Rocks and this sort of thing. When I see he is going to leave, I ask what he proposes to do about me.

It seems he thinks another week or so here and then I can go home again and will be all right. I ask if he remembers the last few weeks or months and what we both said and did.

151

Does he think anything will be different if I just go back again? Andre looks sick and confused as I remind him about what we said and did. He says it wasn't really like that exactly and some things he denies altogether. I think then I must have such a distorted imagination I ought to be locked up. If it is like that, I don't see how I can go back now.

I don't know what to believe. Andre says he has to go and I start to lose my head. Andre says all right then, he will look for a room for me in town as soon as possible, but meanwhile I must just stay here and phone if I want anything.

It is two hours' drive back to Umhlanga Rocks and now he really has to go. So he goes, and here I still am, disconnected in every way.

I don't have my car, or any money, or anyone I can speak to. In fact, I seem to have got myself into worse difficulty than usual and am more confused than usual too.

Do I just write this off as a 'domestic disturbance' like most people have and go home again as if nothing has happened – and then have it happen all over again? Can I? I don't feel as if I can or that I should even try.

Well, I will try to write out the last 15 years for you, Duncan, which will at least make a little more sense. I will try to find someone to post this now (where? I can't see anything here but trees and fields), so at least you will know why I disappeared.

Chapter Fifteen

Wednesday, 23rd January 1975, at Marianhill Mission. I wake up after a very short sleep, feeling sick, desperate, deserted and dirty. Wash yourself then, wash your hair, read your whodunit, finish your letter to Duncan and find someone to post it. Ignore the storm and go to sleep.

I do these things and wake up homesick. I try to speak to Tu [Antonia] then, on the telephone. She is not there. No one is. I wonder what she is thinking and if I should go home.

This room is killing me. I must stop reading whodunits and think about actual life, which is urgent now. I am so desperate because Andre does not understand, or ignores, or forgets. Angry because he will always deny everything and is so much more believable than I am.

I have trouble believing myself these last weeks and so better write everything down as it happens so there can be no mistake. These last months seem to contain everything that went wrong in the last 15 years. So that's another reason to write it down, I think.

Thursday. Andre comes for lunch and we talk about the possible flat on the Esplanade. He is asking, do I really want to move?, so it seems to me. I feel happier and pleased to have seen Andre, although I think he seems upset when he goes away.

Resting before supper, in the now familiar state of conscious sleep, I see my right hand is crawling about on the wall all by itself. Mustn't do that here, or panic, so get up quickly, drink coffee, open the door, stop singing. Shut up!

I telephone Tu, who does not want to talk to me. Andre asks me again, do I really want that flat? He suggests the Osborne Hotel instead. No, I insist.

After supper, sitting dazed in the coffee room, I hear three men discussing the price of cane spirit. Presently one comes over, says he remembers seeing me around with Monty Stafford or Louis Burke. Must have a long memory then, and so what? He is not discouraged. He intends a 'pick up' then? Surely not here?

Basil has eyes like bloodshot ping-pong balls, a Fleet Air Arm pilot's badge on his tie and a phony Canadian accent. He is a most familiar, depressing sort of mess. Will I come out with him to the pub in Pinetown? Certainly I will, but drink does not agree with me and he will have to produce Carnation Milk.

I think we drive through the rain to the Point Yacht Club in Durban and on the way I recall how this sort of conversation with this sort of person is supposed to go, while I watch how this car works in case I need it some time. We sit by the window and I look at the harbour, which I am going to be looking at all the time quite soon now, when I move into the flat on the Esplanade.

Basil relates intimate details of his non-sex life with his wife, who has run away and left him. More details of his sex life with girls he fancies. Every possible detail of his daily sessions at Caesar's Palace.

I recall Zdenka, who worked in such a place, kept me company in Fort Napier, and went mad all over the place in Hillbrow. One evening in my hotel room, she pulled off all her clothes and lay on my bed kicking and screaming terribly.

Timothy, Mama, Dr Brown and I battled to get some clothes on her, got her into Timothy's car, where she threw all her clothes out of the window as they drove along to the hospital. Later she set fire to her room, greeted me at the door with a frying pan ready for anyone else, and the police then took her off to Weskoppies mental hospital to be certified insane and left for good.

I tell Basil that Caesar's Palace sounds amusing. Maybe I will go and work there and see him around. I know this will shut him up.

I say I have changed my mind and will have a drink now, which I don't think will affect me at all under these circumstances except to dull my pain. It does not do anything at all, but Basil disappears into the bar for long enough to get himself really filled up with cane spirit and I am wondering how or if I am going to get anywhere tonight.

Basil has one or two more for the road and we drive off in a blinding deluge, while I think about general astonishment when my remains are found in a car wreck with those of a total stranger, somewhere between the yacht club and Marianhill.

Back in my room, Basil is lounging about on my bed. I am quite certain by now that this poor man would be absolutely harmless in a harem, but tell him it is no use him having hopeful thoughts about

154

my joining him over there. I am fundamentally unwilling, unable, and abnormal in this respect and he had better believe me. Like our maid, Clementine, says every time the iron blows up or something like that: 'It is its nature…'

I read him some of Rod McKuen's poems, which I have here, but they do not register. I read one of my own, which registers far too much. I show him my picture and see that he is going to cry. He looks out of the window a long time and then says: 'Thank you for that. It was what I needed.' He will go away the next day for a few days, which makes me wonder, but I do not ask.

For now, go to bed then, Basil, and cry yourself to sleep. I wish I could cry or sleep, but lie here wondering if this evening showed me anything. Le plus ca change, le plus ca rest, perhaps. No, something has changed a bit, but I do not know what.

Friday. I start to read my story of life from the beginning, in the hope of being able to get on with it. I notice similarities between the worst times and now. Also all the people I have damaged, thinking here I am, still doing it.

Andre phones again about the flat, and says he will take it this afternoon but I must stay here another week. How can I do that and keep any sort of reason intact? Reading Hamlet, I fall asleep for the afternoon, so I suppose there will be no sleep again tonight. Words without thoughts will never go to heaven, but thoughts without feelings are a great deal worse. All I feel is sick and scared.

Saturday. I look 200 years' old this morning and lie on my bed in the conscious sleep, waiting for Andre to come for lunch. He comes at three, looking better. We do not greet each other lovingly and have taken to calling each other by our actual names.

He says Tu is in a very bad temper today and has sent a message that I must come back! Andre looks fed up and, as we talk, we both get angry. He says he does understand me better than I do, but he does not know how to help me.

I am to write out everything that makes it so hard for me to live with him. He does and has always known how desperate I am, but believes I am much better this year because I am beginning to think, instead of just having blind flashes of inspiration.

I am amoral and play a dirty game to get what I want. I am ruthless and selfish. But I am a 'remarkable person'. I am not schizophrenic, paranoic, alcoholic or epileptic. Simply abnormal and without any morals, values or direction.

I ask how he can just go off and leave me in the worst possible states, as he does. Andre is outraged by this. He says I have always been likely to be in such states at any moment and how could he keep me with him all the time? I see this, but would not react the way he does.

We talk about my flat and he looks mad. Andre says I am making mistakes about all of this, but he will only tell me what they are later on. This is enough to make anyone angry.

But he is going to phone Duncan to say what is going on. I feel mad and glad when he has gone. I am strangely elated, making jokes with a nun and nearly going out for a walk.

I wish Duncan would suddenly appear and restore order in my head, but see far too many reasons why he certainly will not. He won't like this whole situation in fact and most likely will disappear into the shadows behind his desk all over again.

So I shall wait here another week in this room and probably go quite mad with the constant changes of mood, hope, fears, beliefs and non-beliefs. I am walking worse and worse, smoking far too much, can hear myself sounding odd when I talk and fear a most horrible night.

I feel I had better write out what Andre wanted me to tell him now and hope it makes sense. I know what's wrong with me anyway. I am an unquiet spirit – and nothing else.

So I write out a whole list of things which bother me about Andre, tear it up in disgust and, hating every bit of it, start again. Andre seems to think that if he gives me material comforts and 'picks me up' when I have fallen over (his example of this is picking me up off Dr Cheetham's lawn after I tried to drown myself), that is what I want to make me happy.

Well, it is not. I want his company, his thoughts, himself to live with, be with – and love. Not to be left alone all the time with my own thoughts and far too many decisions to make on my own.

This goes back a long way, to where I had a baby and no idea what to do with it, for example. The paradox is that he suffocates me all the same and I cannot be my true self in his company. Something absolutely vital is missing between us. The bed, perhaps? I have always felt very bad about that but thought it was a good deal his fault too.

It must be at least 10 years since he ever went to bed before I was asleep and he knows quite well that I can't sleep properly alone. Perhaps I have mistaken ideas about husbands, but I feel that Andre should look after me better, or differently. Perhaps he is 'too masculine', the sort of man I am not used to. Someone once said that I just hate men altogether, but I can't see how that can be true.

I doubt if I am seeing much of this clearly. It is like looking at half a moon and seeing only the dark side, mostly.

Andre is censorious, a teacher all the time. I would rather he just hit me than lecture me, on and on. But the worst is: 'Don't play games with me!' For what possible reason would I want to be an object of pity or contempt? If his needs are not known to me, how can I love him properly by caring about them as much as my own? Why not tell me then? I think he is unfair to me and that I am unfair to him.

I expect him to love me as I am but do not love him as he is. Don't love him at all, then? Well I certainly did once and often still do most extremely, and I cannot bear being disconnected like this now.

Sunday. If I go on throwing up my food like this, I shall surely evaporate altogether. The perpetual electric storms always do make me sick.

In the afternoon, Jay arrives, seems pleased to see me as much as usual and I think I am pleased to see her. But trying to talk sensibly to her is always a strain because she keeps on sort of coming and going and I must be sure not to upset her in any way.

Jay says that Duncan is coming here to see me on Wednesday at four o' clock. She says it several times, so maybe I look as if nothing is sinking in. I don't think anything did much, until after she had gone.

What I think this evening is that if Duncan does come on Wednesday and wants me to go home, then I will go at once and hope that he will help me manage it somehow. Otherwise I will still go to the flat. If this happened right now, I would go right now, but what will I think by Wednesday? It seems it could be absolutely anything.

Monday. After lunch, I try to induce the conscious sleep that is often restful, and find that I can. But I feel my head is very sore, my insides full of splintered glass, and my left is arm waving about in the air.

Better go right to sleep then, but someone in the chair right beside me says 'Hilary', very loud and clear. This is too much altogether, especially since it is not any voice I know. I get up and go downstairs to find Basil, who has returned and is hiding behind his dark glasses, fairly sober.

Tuesday. It is very difficult to think about anything important. I had best go to that flat on the Esplanade, and hope it won't be for too long, but I am beginning to enjoy being alone. I talk to poor Mrs Lallos, who is still living through the Hungarian revolution and seldom well enough to get up at all.

Andre is coming for supper tonight and I do wish I could think, but wish much more that I could feel – anything other than pain. If I don't cry soon, I fear horrible consequences.

Andre looks ill, confused and rather vacant. His clothes are unpressed and rather dirty. I forgot to cut his hair before I left, so it is very wild. We are disconnected and I believe he really wants me not to go home. He has forgotten that he asked me to write anything and says he can't think but only feel. He says he just feels sad.

It seems to me I may have made him worse by going than by staying at home. He is talking about getting a flat for us all, but not making any sense.

It seems Tu is not missing me and I suppose I have lost her altogether. Better so for her.

Andre says Duncan may not visit because it is so far from Durban to Marianhill and he is so busy he is unlikely to be able to take the afternoon off. I can take this two ways: either I must feel bad about it or be prepared for nothing to happen tomorrow. Who knows?

All I know is Andre and I are both sick and not making any sense at all. My poor Tu had better have me sick than absent, as she said she would prefer. Andre can't possibly look after her.

Wednesday. The funny nun – I call her 'meshugga' – brings an enormous Bavarian Mother Superior from Greytown to have lunch with me. Better practise sensible conversation then and see if that works.

Her nuns are all African, so I ask which wins between the superstitions of Darkest Africa and Holy Rome? This question brings much animation and gets us through lunch. It seems Darkest Africa wins hands down.

I put myself right out by mistake after lunch and wake up to find Duncan actually and miraculously outside my door, looking and behaving exactly like himself.

Shock and thankfulness defeat such wits as I have and I can't remember anything I have to say at all. I wish I could just sit here, enjoy his company and talk about something pleasant for once. But presently the room settles down and becomes quiet.

I show Duncan the picture I have here, remember some of what I have to say, and hear what he is saying to me. I know I'm going to panic if he leaves me here but if I can get outside that should be better. It is much better, and Duncan disappears gradually – a waving hand from the car, which is most truly considerate.

This room is habitable now and I will stop thinking and see what is to be seen here until Sunday.

Downstairs in the corridor, holding himself up by a doorpost, is Basil. How are you Basil? Plastered. We sit in the coffee room where Basil thinks he is having coffee, which has been finished long ago, and talks a lot of nonsense about women, much too loud.

Come on, Basil. Let's go to bed. Which unfortunate remark leads to an argument, ending in him talking loudly about what he would like to do with a nun here tonight and me losing my temper altogether. You be quiet and hear me now. Any nun here could and would push you over with one finger at any time. You are so stupid you give yourself away every time you open your mouth, swallow endless fortified vitamin E capsules and liver-restoring pills, or make endless talk about Caesar's Palace, which is the last resort for senile old goats. You have simply drunk yourself incapable and can't even see how obvious you are. Even your accent keeps slipping and you are nearly blind. You better listen or soon you won't have a shoulder left to cry on except another mess like mine.

This results in a long and painful silence from Basil. Then he looks oddly relieved and says I am absolutely right. He sees that I am a completely different person tonight and asks me please to tell him what to do.

Go far away and be a game ranger, right now, before you change your mind. How did I know that is what he wants to be? Do I have second sight? No, I see your badge and chance to know some things about the minds of airmen.

Basil says he had to sell all his guns a little while ago and now wants to go off to bed and have a good cry, so I help him upstairs to his room. Do I know what he is going to feel like around 12 o' clock? Yes, I do know very well. Then please, for simple kindness and humanity, come and see me then if you are awake too.

All right then, if I am awake I will come and hold your hand. But to my shame and dead against the only general principle I have, I stay in my room and leave him to die his horrible death a little more, alone.

Who wants most ought to get it, no matter what. But now I can't even stick to that. Unstuck and sunk altogether, then. Stop thinking – and go to sleep.

Thursday: Sitting in the sun outside the front door I feel so well, I phone Duncan to tell him this in case I worried him. The meshugga nun comes to talk, saying something about my visitor yesterday. She thought he was Greek and was my brother. She must think we both look Greek then? Impossible.

I am about to ask if she has ever considered how much better life would be if we could choose how we were born, and how much better life would be if one could choose one's own relations. But that would be a mistake.

She is bound to think one should be absolutely satisfied with relations provided by God. This thought takes me down the road into the chapel. I cannot find the perfectly obvious door until someone takes me right to it.

Sitting there, looking around at Sister Pientia's paintings and decorations everywhere, I find them to be crude, badly drawn and rather commercial. They can't be the same I saw years ago and so liked. Jesus, hanging up there on a heavily-decorated cross, looks like a bad-tempered dummy, which offends me. There is nothing here for me at all, so I walk off down the road again towards the big African church.

I watch myself walking along this road like a movie unwinding. Last time I took a walk like this was in Umhlanga Rocks, along to the lagoon and into the sea. I shall never understand what was so frightfully wicked about trying to drown myself when after all I belong to no one. I should be allowed to die in peace, surely. But not in public. Not here.

The Zulu church is incredibly ornate and barren at the same time. But it has a nice floor of broken bricks. I look at every single thing here, find nothing, and walk off again towards the monastery. It looks miles away and if I get there I shall not get back, being suddenly exhausted. But I do get back and lie on the floor under the bed to get cool.

At lunch, I see Mrs Lallos is sitting somewhere else and here is the 'meshugga' nun again with another nun for me. I wonder what is in her mind?

This time it's a French nun, Sister Veronique. I ask her what her real name is. Monique. She is laughing, and tells me all about Saint Veronique and why she chose her name. What a lovely story.

She tells me all about Saint Augustine then, which is absolutely fascinating. A more progressive saint than Benedict, she says. She has come here for peace, to write a thesis about friendship, Augustine and philosophy. I am confused but hope she has not nearly finished and will stay.

This afternoon, I have been thinking about Andre and Tu with much love and pain. Most unbearable is the thought of Tu dancing for me in her red tights and jersey in the evenings when we are alone at home. She is so beautiful, like a little gipsy wild girl with all that hair, dancing like mad and laughing all the time.

Andre doesn't like it. Says she is showing off – and what about her homework? He doesn't like her music either. He prefers Beethoven to Tu then, hurts her feelings with this and makes us both mad.

It makes me sad, because he misses so much of Tu. Misses the whole point of her true self and only approves if she is something else, just as he does with me. I remember that I used to think being yourself is a luxury one should not expect. I had better think about that tonight.

Andre phones after supper and I say I will phone back. But I lie on my bed too sick to move for so long that he phones back again. He goes on and on about the difficulties of moving me from here and I hear myself getting to sound odd.

What can I do about moving myself from here? Andre sounds hysterical and I speak to Tu, who sounds odd as well. Is anything wrong there? Andre tries to say, not really, but I am sure something has happened and I hear him shouting at Tu to be quiet.

It is long after midnight and I am so worried and sure I am doing the wrong thing. Why leave me to simply guess at an answer for us all?

Friday morning, there is Veronique who joins me in drinking coffee on the verandah. What does she think about Africa? The truth – although I can see she feels she should not say it – is Africa is absolutely the most bitter end. The political situation here defeats her altogether, though she is fortunate in having a multi-racial convent.

She talks about the psychology of black children who she says cannot be given any motivation because no one wants them or loves them or ever will – and who can be motivated to anything without love? I think how very truly loving she is herself, giving me all her thoughts and company like this, when what she came for was to work in peace.

We talk about the war. Veronique's home was in Dunkirk, she is exactly the same age as me, and what she leaves out I can imagine very well. We talk all morning and through lunch, where I bring a photograph of Duncan's painting to show her. No comment about this, but she looks thoughtful.

A friend phones, but I will not answer. The meshugga nun is very funny about having to tell the friend she cannot see me anywhere. She says to me: 'Go zen! Qvick! Run, vere I really can't see you!' She points dramatically down the corridor and I disappear into the nearest loo.

At suppertime and afterwards on the cool, dark veranda, Veronique and I talk on and on. We go up to the attic and look at the night from there. We go into the little chapel here, which is warm and beautiful.

She gives me explanations of things I don't understand in the Bible. She says I have got the wrong Bible, which explains nothing. She agrees Pientia Salhort's paintings are deplorable and teutonic, so I was not having distorted thoughts about that. Later, when the chapel is closed, we sit in my room where I know she waits with love and patience for me to tell her what is wrong.

So I tell her the entire predicament that I am in, in general and right now. I wonder what she guessed of this and she says I was doing all right, not showing anything. It was the photograph – of the 'tragic painting' – that told her something was very wrong.

I tell her why I painted this and am astonished to find she knows Duncan very well. She is astonished too and very funny about him. Says she was 'terrified' of him! Well, he only terrified me once and I can't imagine Veronique provoking anything like that. It seems it was the 'forthright' and 'unpriestly' manner, shaking up inattentive students, that surprised her. We talk about psychology then, and various books we read.

Veronique says I would like The Confessions of Saint Augustine, even though I can't read Latin, so I will try that one day soon. She says my situation with Andre surely is not unusual, which is about the most restoring remark anyone has made to me yet. I am exhausted but almost happy and most relieved.

I know what Veronique is doing for me. She is restoring me to a state of loving, in which I can love Andre again, see everything straighter and come back to life. She simply wraps me in love. But will it stick? We have to leave on Sunday. Never on Sunday. Go to sleep. Lie on your hand. Shut up. There is still tomorrow and maybe this won't fade.

Saturday. Feeling more dead than alive, I try to sleep on and off all day, doing nothing. Around five things improve.

I find the 'meshugga' nun has new shoes which hurt and she intends to throw them away. Good for you, but don't throw away everything you have, which will hurt more.

Andre phones to say he has moved most of my things. He sounds calmer but as if he is leaving a lot out. I fear there is trouble with Tu and hear myself getting to sound odd.

It upsets me just to talk to Andre, every time. I intend to phone Tu and explain this is only for six months while Andre looks for a house in town where we shall all be together again. I want to put her mind at rest.

I believe this is what will happen, I shall recover myself this way and be able to start again. But I do not do it – I tell Veronique I lost the 'envie' and was afraid I might sound confused. We sit talking on the quiet veranda until bedtime and now I am expecting to sleep, feeling calm and restored again, although painful.

163

Sunday. Refreshed, optimistic and determined to go on. I must regain my individual self, although I still can't bear to think of Tu dancing. I can't bear living with her treating me with contempt either.

Andre phones twice to put off the time he will fetch me. Veronique leaves early, but has given me her address, which I am sure I am going to need. I leave Marianhill at four o' clock with Andre and say good-bye to dear 'meshugga meshugga'. She holds my hand so hard I am astonished, says it has been a pleasure for her, that I do not look any better and that she will pray for me.

Arriving at the Esplanade flat, I am dead already. Andre looks and sounds dead also and has nothing to say except he has said too much all these years, has nothing more to say and has no plans at all.

He is overburdened with work, while the finances seem to be his worst problem. I am convinced he is going to keep me here quite helpless with no money for punishment, which he believes in. I've had enough of that already I should think, all of my life.

I am too tired to unpack, but do it anyway and try to eat something. The noise of the city is deafening. The heat is unbearable. Splintered glass not only now, but a great big lump of ice as well. I am absolutely terrified. What am I doing here? What has happened? What have I done? Frying in hell, I suppose. Bang, bang, bang, all down the stairs... shock after shock, and here I am now at the bottom of the well. Not well. Most unwell, in fact. Shut up.

Monday. It takes me nearly five hours to get up and get dressed, which is absurd. Tired, I suppose, but I walk easier if there is no one watching. There is blood all over my foot but no cut that I can see.

Andre comes in the afternoon, looking and sounding fed up. He says he feels sick. Clem is still away and everything is in a mess. I ask if he would like to come here for weekends while I go home and see to that, but he says no.

The flat is too noisy for him. The windows are soundproofed, so leave the door open and the fan on, like I do. No. So it can't be like that. Is he just stupid? I can't see him at all now and am sure I have done all this wrong.

Tuesday. Why am I so slowed up? I nearly miss the bus to see Duncan at Warman House [the alcohol and drug treatment centre], but it gets me there too soon anyway.

Nothing here seems real but I think I am clear enough in what I have to say, which is mostly I wish Duncan can find out what Andre thinks and tell me what to do. But he will not get the truth, which I know but cannot say. No one can.

Duncan has said the worst times for me are over – and these were the years with Wolf and Vere. Well, we all loved each other, that I can understand, and Vere said I was the most truly gallant person he had every known. Not gallant enough to stay with either of them though, was I? I can't follow this thought or what Duncan really means.

Back at the flat, I think I have sunstroke and had better go to sleep. Andre comes at six and I fall to pieces at once, mostly from pain.

He is nice and looks better, but if I'm going to feel like this every time I see him then I'd better not see him until I feel better. I find one Seconal in my jacket and try now to sleep with that. I can't even begin to think why any of this has happened and wish it would stop.

Wednesday. I wake up ill and know I will never get to that bus today. I go out to look for a phone box and people are staring at me because I am not walking right.

In the call box, I phone some man to say I cannot come. But I put the phone down on the phonebook, which is wrong. I pick it up again and hear someone who sounds like Duncan talking to some other man, so I put it back in the cradle, right I hope, and go to look for cigarettes and pens.

I want to write to my cousin Simon in England. Back in my room, I lock the door, close the window, and lie down because I am crying. I try the half-sleep, but cry on and on. This is the worst day yet during this time.

I feel mad and look mad, making faces at myself in the mirror and screaming. Remember to shut that window and stop falling. You will hurt yourself. Singing that song again all day, on and off. Well, the song is right anyway.

I must not see anyone at all until this is all over, one way or the other. Just cry and cry and give up. I am so afraid of that window. I will throw everything here out of it instead and so get locked up, which is where I ought to be. In prison.

There is absolutely nothing left in the world I can do about anything. Maybe start to walk back along the beach and so into the sea, which was warm and beautiful. Or maybe ask Jack to lock me up for human kindness. But he is not a police chief any more I think and probably he has gone mad again and gone.

Someone just knocked on my door looking for someone and I spoke to him in French. He answered me in French and looked astonished. Too many coincidences for me lately. Is one going to save me yet again? Perhaps if I lie here very still.

I want to go home. Or have shocks, or Pentothal, or morphia. I just want to be unconscious. Wonder why I don't want to drink any more, even today. But I feel much drunker all this time, without anything mostly, ever since what happened in October. Which must have been awful.

If I throw everything out, I will get shut up like Zdenka. The sun went down long ago, the wind came up, it's raining now and I have gone to bed.

Tomorrow I will find a plan, get locked up, get rest, go home. No, I can't do that in this state. It seems to be taking a very long time this time and I have no chance at all – so die like a sick monkey, here alone. Or so I hope. But you did, didn't you?

Well it is not two o' clock yet and maybe I will feel better in the morning. I have sealed up all the last that I wrote and all I want no one to see, to be destroyed, unread. But I leave this book on my desk I suppose, for academic interest, and maybe someone will listen to someone else sometime.

Thursday. It seems that I shall cry again today and not be able to do anything, like yesterday. Why not write to Simon, instead of this? But he is probably doing the same thing, since identical twins always do. Poor Simon.

I recall Papa's most common remark, all of my life: 'Paddle your own canoe, dear. Paddle your own canoe'. And every time I capsize there is a lot of fuss while he pays the doctor's bill. Andre's view is exactly the same, so I suppose they have this in common. I think if two people are in one canoe they do better if they both paddle. Obviously.

Writing this, I feel anger, tears coming, pain. I will ask for no more help from anyone then, unless I really need it. But if I ever do, I will be too angry with whoever left me here to this, like this, watching to see if I do drown or not.

'Laugh and the world laughs with you' has made me more angry than anything else in my life and everyone still does it to me. On the other hand, when you do the right thing and feel well, and don't need to rely on help, everyone watches and waits to see what you will do next.

I suppose I am expected to fall on my face and scream for help, so I can be picked up, reproved for wickedness and sent back to the dogbox again. Think again. I go out of that window first and it is this that will drive me to it.

So now Andre can most likely scrape what's left of me from the Esplanade under this window, Duncan can preside over my funeral, my friends will shake their heads in sorrow. But Tu – Tu is probably why this did not happen yesterday or today yet – but it was so near. A second's impulse only. Anger is saving me again.

Andre says I only see things in black or white, while he sees things in different shades of grey. Dismal thought. Rod McKuan says: 'A heart's bright red shades are easier to hit than some black, crouched target. Even if I could, I wouldn't have it any other way.' I wouldn't either. Who wants a grey picture?

I'm going to write a fairy story now, about a penguin that I see, black and white. The very last penguin on the very last ice floe in the middle of the Frozen North. But the ice moves, so what is going to happen? Wolf always told me: 'Nothing happens – only you happen.' I saw what he meant but it is not so for me. Put out the light and see what happens to that penguin.

I can't taste iodine anymore, so that is something anyway.

Friday. Last night I walked around and around this room with so much pain, I heard myself laughing about it. Best thing to do, I think.

An alarm bell kept on ringing at intervals and a cockroach ran up my arm, so I pulled the whole bed to bits but could not find it. I wondered if I had imagined both and in the early morning slept an hour or two.

No more iodine today – and I think maybe the worst is over.

Afterword
Antonia Gialerakis

After just over a month in the flat on The Esplanade, Hilary returned home to my father and me.

We later moved from Umhlanga Rocks to Essenwood Road, Durban, where we lived for ten years. My mother continued to paint and held another exhibition of her work.

I left home for London in 1986 and my parents later divorced. My father remarried and retired to Crete with his wife Patti.

Hilary eventually returned to Marianhill where she lived peacefully with the nuns, until finally moving to a nursing home in Pinetown. She died in 2003 after being admitted to hospital for a routine hernia operation, during which doctors discovered advanced and inoperable cancer.

This work is a tribute to my mother's memory. May she rest in peace.

Acknowledgements

I would like to acknowledge the following for their help with my initial self-publishing of this book in 2008: Roger Smith, for his contribution to the Foreword and his dedicated and patient help with the final editing of the manuscript; my father Andre Gialerakis, for his input on dates and facts and for his unquestioning support of this project; Gerardine Killeen, for her advice, love and for propping me up when the going got rough; John Kevan, who sadly died before he could see this work come to fruition, for his advice and guidance regarding facts, dates, times and places; Lee Kevan, for her continued support; Vernon 'Little Werner' Reynolds for his advice on self-publishing; Angela Casey; and everyone else who has contributed to research throughout the five years I have worked on this project.

Thank you to Janie Ironside Wood, who, in early 2012, brought this book to the attention of Naim Attallah, Chairman of Quartet Books. It has been an arduous yet rewarding journey towards my meeting with Naim, who I would most sincerely like to thank for recognising that this is indeed a story worth telling.